Professional Development for Teachers

Teaching and Assessing Skills in Economics

AF841408

Susan Grant

CAMBRIDGE
UNIVERSITY PRESS

CAMBRIDGE
UNIVERSITY PRESS

University Printing House, Cambridge CB2 8BS, United Kingdom

Cambridge University Press is part of the University of Cambridge.

It furthers the University's mission by disseminating knowledge in the pursuit of education, learning and research at the highest international levels of excellence.

www.cambridge.org
Information on this title: www.cambridge.org/9780521548250

© University of Cambridge International Examinations 2006

This publication is in copyright. Subject to statutory exception and to the provisions of relevant collective licensing agreements, no reproduction of any part may take place without the written permission of Cambridge University Press.

First published 2006

A catalogue record for this publication is available from the British Library

ISBN 978-0-521-54825-0 Paperback

Cambridge University Press has no responsibility for the persistence or accuracy of URLs for external or third-party internet websites referred to in this publication, and does not guarantee that any content on such websites is, or will remain, accurate or appropriate.

Every effort has been made to reach copyright holders. The publishers would be pleased to hear from anyone whose rights they have unwittingly infringed.

Contents

Foreword

Teaching is a complex and demanding profession. All over the world, societies change in response to new knowledge gained, technological developments, globalisation and a requirement for an ever-more sophisticated and educated population. Teachers are in the forefront of such social change, responding with speed and confidence to the new demands made of them, in terms of both their knowledge and the way in which they teach. This series is intended to help them in adapting to these changes and in their professional development as teachers.

Curriculum changes worldwide are putting increased emphasis on the acquisition of skills as well as subject knowledge, so that students will have the ability to respond flexibly to the swiftly changing modern environment. As a result, teachers must be able both to teach and assess skills and to adjust their own teaching methods to embrace a wider range of techniques for both teaching and assessing in the classroom. The books in this series are practical handbooks which explore these techniques and offer advice on how to use them to enhance the teacher's own practice.

The handbooks are written by teachers with direct experience of teaching and assessing skills at this level. We have asked them to write for their readers in such a way that the readers feel directly supported in their professional development. Thus in this book there are tasks for students, there are tasks for teachers, pauses for reflection and questions to be answered. We hope that readers will find that this mixture of the practical and the professional helps them, both in their practice and in their own sense of what it means to be an effective teacher in this modern, changing world of international education.

Dr Kate Pretty
Series Editor

Acknowledgements

I am much indebted to Jamuna Acharya. She provided me with many useful insights and helpful suggestions. My thanks also go to Mark Dowling and Camilla Erskine for their perceptive comments and encouragement.

1 Introduction

The work of economists influences people's lives in far more ways than most of them realise. Their theories and advice to governments, organisations and firms can contribute to lowering unemployment, raising incomes and creating a better environment. Economists can change the world!

Throughout the twentieth century the number of Economics courses, books and articles and of economists increased dramatically. There are signs that this rapid expansion will continue in the twenty-first century. Access to more and more economic analysis and debate is becoming available to both economists and the general public through articles published in newspapers, magazines and on the Internet, and through television and radio programmes. Many people, nevertheless, remain uncertain about what the study of Economics involves. As a teacher, you will have to define Economics and explain the role of economists.

As Economics is sometimes an optional subject, you may also have to talk to younger, prospective students about the benefits of studying the subject. I also recap these benefits at the start of the course. I find this relatively easy as I genuinely believe that Economics is an important and interesting subject that can change lives. It combines well with a number of other subjects, including Business Studies, Geography, History and Mathematics. A wide range of skills can be developed through the study of Economics. Its strengths are recognised by many professions, and students with Economics qualifications are recruited into – for instance – accountancy, finance, journalism, law and management. Some of your students may go on to become economists. Now is a good time to specialise in Economics. There is a world shortage of economists and good economists can expect to be recruited to stimulating and well-paid jobs.

As well as benefiting individual students through the skills, interest and greater earning potential they can gain, the study of Economics benefits the wider society. An understanding of Economics makes students more effective and more productive members of society.

Economists can also significantly improve people's living standards. I compare Economics to Medicine. In both cases, students have to learn a range of technical terms, use these terms precisely, examine how a healthy body (economy) should work, explore what can go wrong with it and why, and make suggestions for improving it.

In my first lesson, I discuss with students some of the issues that economists explore. These include the following:

- How can poverty be reduced?
- Should health care be provided free of charge?
- Why are the citizens of the United States richer than those of India?
- Why will China soon be the world's most powerful economy?
- Should footballers be paid more than nurses?
- Why does the price of oil fluctuate so much?

Teacher activity 1.1

Produce a leaflet for younger students explaining the advantages of studying Economics.

Purpose of the book

This book is intended to identify some of the key skills Economics students need to develop, and to provide ideas on teaching strategies, advice on assessment and guidance on preparation for examinations. It is aimed at teachers of 14–16-year-old Economics students, using the University of Cambridge International Examinations (CIE) IGCSE and O Level syllabuses as examples.

The ideas in the book can be adapted for use with different levels of examination and students of different ages.

There are many ways of teaching Economics and this book is not aiming to be prescriptive. What it is seeking to do is to provide suggestions on teaching approaches and assessment strategies.

I recognise that the resources and experience of teachers and the abilities and motivation of their students vary. For example, you may be a newly qualified teacher or a teacher of many years' experience. You may be one of a group of teachers of Economics, or you may be the only teacher of the subject in your school – and have no one with whom to talk over your ideas and experience.

What all Economics teachers, however, are likely to have in common is the desire to find new ways of improving their students' learning experience. As an Economics teacher you also probably review your course materials and learning activities more frequently than other teachers as your subject matter is constantly changing.

I hope this book will give you a number of insights and ideas that you can use in your teaching.

Contents

This first chapter, as well as outlining the purpose and content of the book, explains the benefits of studying Economics and identifies some of the key elements of effective teaching in Economics.

Chapter 2 starts by exploring key skills for Economics students to develop. Economics students need to be able to think logically, to write clearly, to interpret and use figures, to be up to date with current affairs, and to draw diagrams.

Chapter 3 discusses how you might interpret the syllabus and use it as the basis for your course planning. It also touches on some teaching strategies.

In Chapter 4 teaching strategies are explored in more depth. The focus is on active learning. A number of ways of promoting active learning are explored, with suggestions for how you might employ these. Chapters 5–7 concentrate on the skills needed and assessment used in the main types of papers students sit.

To take advantage of the skills they have developed, students need to do well in the examination papers. Chapter 8 provides some suggestions for activities you can use, and advice you can give students on how they can improve their revision and examination preparation.

Chapter 9 examines some of the resources you may draw on in developing your course and delivering your lessons.

Throughout the book, I have tried to place the emphasis on information and advice that I hope will make your lessons relevant, interesting and productive.

Key elements of effective teaching in Economics

Effective teaching in Economics, as in all subjects, needs careful planning. This involves not only planning teaching content and teaching strategy, but also assessment and preparation for external examinations.

In planning these stages it is important to build in some flexibility, and also not to underestimate the time needed at the start of the course to introduce students to the subject and towards the end of the course to undertake revision.

Teachers of all subjects have to consider how to keep their students motivated and how to develop their skills. They also need to ensure that they will do well in examinations. This last objective, however, has to be pursued carefully. There is a risk of the focus becoming too narrow, with students selecting to learn only what they consider necessary to answer examination questions. By encouraging students to learn beyond the demands of the examination, you are likely to allow them to develop their interests, make them more aware of the links between topics and, indeed, to make them more capable of answering examination questions phrased in a slightly different way.

On occasion, a didactic approach may be used in teaching Economics. Such an approach involves the teacher formally explaining topics and students listening. On most occasions, however, teaching strategies that encourage active learning are the most productive. This book focuses on teaching strategies that promote active learning.

LOOKING BACK

You may now want to reflect on the following questions:

- Are you looking for new ways of improving your students' learning experience and performance?
- How do you encourage students to study Economics?
- What opportunities exist to use a variety of teaching strategies in your lessons?
- Do you use many real-world examples in your teaching?

2 The key skills of an economist

The famous economist John Maynard Keynes described, more than 70 years ago, the skills that a 'master economist' must possess:

> He must reach a high standard in several different directions and must combine talents not often found together. He must be mathematician, historian, statesman, philosopher – in some degree. He must understand symbols and speak in words. He must contemplate the particular in terms of the general, and touch abstract and concrete in the same flight of thought. He must study the present in the light of the past for the purposes of the future. No part of man's nature or his institutions must lie entirely outside his regard.
>
> *Essays in Biography, The Collected Writings of John Maynard Keynes*, vol. X, Royal Economic Society, Macmillan Press Ltd, 1972.

This is an ambitious and also an inspiring list. It gives an indication of the skills that Economics students need to gain. They have to communicate quite complex ideas and theories in a clear manner, undertake numerical calculations, and interpret data presented in a variety of forms. They also have to analyse and evaluate economic problems and solutions, interpret and use diagrams, and employ ICT (Information and Communications Technology) skills.

In developing these skills, it is useful to apply a variety of teaching approaches and activities. Variety increases student motivation, and different students are likely to respond well to different activities.

As students' skills develop, they will find the subject increasingly more comprehensible and rewarding. They will learn to think as an economist and to use the tools of an economist.

Oral communication

Developing candidates' oral communication increases their confidence, makes it more likely that they will ask when they do not understand something, helps them to formulate ideas and arguments, and enables them to learn from each other.

Question-and-answer sessions

These are a simple and effective way of promoting oral skills that can be used throughout the course. They are a good way of checking at the start and end of a lesson students' ability to recall key points, and they can be used during the lesson to assess understanding. They also permit differentiation as more searching questions can be directed to the more able students and more straightforward questions to the less able students.

Class discussions

These can help to develop oral communication skills, but they have to be carefully planned to avoid the discussions drifting and to ensure that all students are involved. To achieve this, students can be given briefing sheets with discussion points and, on occasion, can be divided into smaller groups, with representatives from each group reporting back findings to the class.

Role playing and simulations

These can be used to develop not only oral skills but also data interpretation and writing skills. Students often respond very positively to such activities. They enable students to understand the factors influencing economic decisions, provide variety in classroom activities, and again generate opportunities for differentiation.

Presentations

Requiring students to give presentations is another way of advancing their oral and writing skills. Students can be asked to research a topic individually, in pairs or in groups, and then to present their findings to the class. Presentations can also enable students to make use of visual and ICT equipment.

Teacher activity 2.1

Arrange some simulation exercises for students, for example:

- **The budget** The roles could include government officials, company directors, journalists, pensioners and public workers. Briefing notes could be given to each participant about the state of the economy and their situation. Government officials and their advisers could be asked to draw up and present a simplified budget. The other participants could be asked first for what they want from the budget and then for their reaction to the budget.
- **Starting up a business** The roles could include entrepreneur(s), business advisers, rival firms, bankers and consumers. Those setting up the business and their advisers could consider what factors would influence whether the business will be successful, the type of business organisation to operate, and what their strategies will be. Bankers could be asked what factors will influence whether they will lend to the company and what conditions they might impose; rival firms, how they will react to the entry of the new company into the market; and consumers, whether they would switch to the new company's products.
- **The government as an employer** The government is planning to open a new hospital. The roles may include government officials, employers in a private-sector hospital, trade-union representatives, skilled workers (e.g. doctors) and unskilled workers (e.g. porters). Government officials could be asked to consider job specifications and salaries in order to draw up an advertisement. Private-sector employers could be required to consider the effect on their recruitment and to prepare a report on how they will respond. Trade-union representatives could be asked to consider how they would encourage the new employees to join them and to draw up a list of benefits the workers would gain on joining. The workers could be set the task of considering what factors might have influenced their choice of occupation and what will determine whether they will apply for jobs at the new hospital.
- **Money** A country experiences hyper-inflation. The government withdraws the country's paper money and coins. It meets to decide what form of money to use (e.g. gold, sea shells, leather strips and playing cards). Each group should consider to what extent a particular asset has the characteristics of money and how effective it would be in carrying out the functions of money.

Student activity 2.1

Each member of the class is given responsibility for noting developments in a particular aspect of the economy or an industry, and reporting back to the class at regular intervals.

Written communication

To answer examination questions in a relevant and lucid manner, it is obviously important not only that students understand the concepts they are discussing but also that they have good language skills and feel confident in using Economics terms.

There is a variety of ways of seeking to develop students' ability to write Economics answers in a clear and relevant way. Encouraging them to read widely, including extracts from textbooks and articles in Economics magazines and newspapers, should expose them to good writing and a variety of writing styles.

To increase the accuracy of their written work, students could be asked to produce their own Economics dictionary. When they come across an Economics term, they can add it to their dictionary with an appropriate definition. You should check the definitions regularly.

An accurate dictionary and clear notes can be used by students to inform their answers. Most students are likely to need advice on note-taking. (See pages 9–12.)

Worksheets are particularly useful in developing understanding of the subject and written skills. At the start of the course these can concentrate on short-answer questions assessing knowledge, understanding and application. If students have limited English-language skills, early worksheets can require students to select the appropriate words to use to fill in gaps.

As the course progresses, these worksheets can become more demanding, requiring longer answers and assessing not only knowledge, understanding and application, but also analysis, judgement and decision-making.

Partway through the course students can be introduced to past examination questions. In providing guidance to students on how they answer questions, it is important to emphasise that they should pay particular attention to the directive words in questions. As examination reports stress:

> To gain the highest marks in questions that ask for a discussion, candidates should present more than one side of an argument and then come to a conclusion. They should also be prepared to present their own view of the matter . . . They should decide whether, for example, the advantages outweigh the disadvantages, or the case for a given change mentioned in the question is greater than the case against. They should then clearly state what they conclude.

Note-taking

Note-taking is an important written communication skill and one which should be seen as part of active learning. An ability to take good-quality notes from a variety of sources including lessons, books and television programmes will help a student progress through the course and stand them in good stead for the future.

Notes serve a number of purposes, including identifying key points, analysing data and providing information for classwork, homework and revision purposes.

Many students waste time and effort writing down everything a teacher says and every word from a section of a textbook to very little purpose. In practice you are likely to have to help students develop their note-taking skills.

You could start by giving them some advice, including:

- record the source of the notes and the date;
- take notes for a specific purpose;
- think about what you are hearing or reading;
- consider what information you need – be selective;
- write concisely;
- use your own words where possible;
- write clearly;
- leave plenty of space so other points can be added later;
- use headings and subheadings;
- use lettering and numbering schemes;
- emphasise key points with underlining, highlighters and capitals;
- include diagrams where appropriate;
- use abbreviations for common words and for Economics terms.

You could explain that, whilst linear notes are the most common way of making notes, there may be occasions when students may wish to use tables, flow diagrams or spider diagrams. Figure 2.1 is a spider diagram that summarises some of the key points about diagrams.

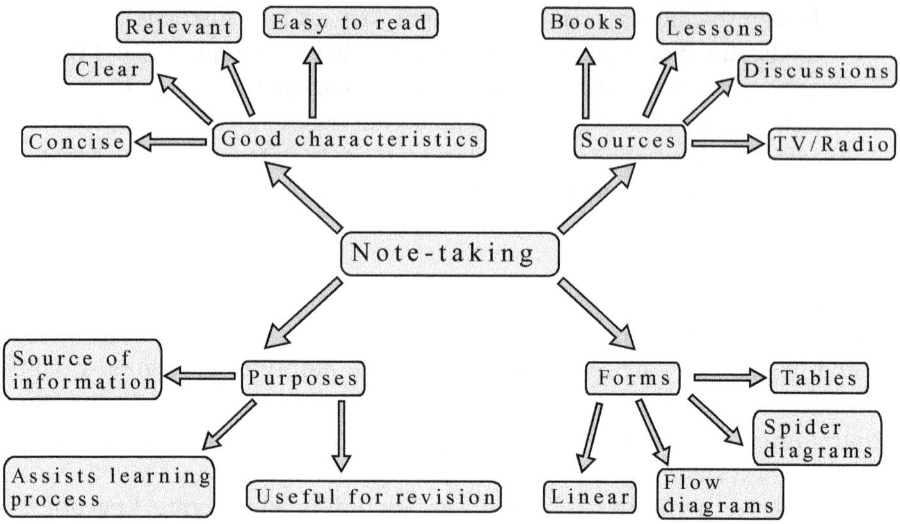

Figure 2.1: Spider diagram

Then you could show them examples of good and bad note-taking. For example, the following extract could be used for notes on gender imbalance in China.

Example 2.1: Note-taking

China, the most populous nation on Earth, could find itself dealing with the combined frustrations of as many as 40 million single men by 2020 because of its one-child policy in creating a shortage of female babies.

In an unusually frank speech on China's looming demographic crisis, Li Weixiong, who advises the country's political consultative conference on population issues, said a cultural preference for boys was creating an artificial disparity between the number of boys and girls that represents 'a serious threat to building a well-off society'.

Mr Li said the gender ratio had stayed relatively normal until 1982 – two years after the Chinese authorities imposed the one-child rule – at 100 girls born for every 108 boys. But by 2000, the ratio had shifted significantly to about 117 boys to 100 girls. The disparity is even bigger in rural areas, where the boy-to-girl imbalance is estimated to be as high as 130 to 100.

Abortions are not the only cause of the imbalance. There is alarming evidence that the intense pressure on couples to make sure their child is a boy has prompted a resurgence of female infanticide, despite attempts to stamp out the centuries-old practice.

Rural families are said to be particularly tempted to kill female off-spring, such is the pressure to produce a child capable of coping with the physical demands of farming and prevent cash-strapped farming households from being plunged even deeper into poverty.

In some cases, according to reports, other girls are hidden from the authorities or die at a young age from neglect.

Even in urban areas, boys are generally preferred because they are regarded as more able than girls to provide for their families, care for elderly relatives and continue the family line.

Extract from '40m bachelors and no women . . . the birth of a new problem for China', by Justin McCurry and Rebecca Allison, *The Guardian*, page 3, 9 March 2004.

Bad note-taking

China is the most populous country. It could have 40m single men by 2020 because of its one-child policy which is creating a shortage of female babies.

Li Weixiong, who advises the country's political consultative conference on population issues, said that there were too many boys because of cultural preference. Gender ratio was relatively normal up to 1982 (108 boys for every 100 girls) but by 2000 it changed to 117 boys to 100 girls. Bigger disparity in rural areas where it is 130 boys to 100 girls.

Imbalance is caused not just by abortions. The pressure on couples to make sure their only child is a boy has resulted in a resurgence of infanticide.

Rural families are particularly tempted to kill girls because of the need for boys for farm work. Some girls are hidden from the authorities and some die due to neglect. Even in urban areas boys are preferred as more able to provide for families, care for elderly relatives and continue the family line.

In this case the note-taking has essentially involved copying down all but a few of the original words. The time has been spent writing, rather than thinking about and ordering the information. The notes are neither easy to refer to nor easy to remember.

Good note-taking

Gender imbalance in China

The problem

Too few girls being born. Government policy introduced in 1980 = families can only have

one child. They are opting for boys.
1982 ratio = 108 boys:100 girls
2000 ratio = 117 boys:100 girls (130:100 in rural areas)

Ways used to ensure 1 child = boy
1. abortions
2. murder of baby girls – especially in rural areas
3. neglect of baby girls

Reasons why boys preferred
1. thought more capable of manual work
2. expected to have higher earnings – more capable of supporting elderly relatives
3. will continue family line
Source: Guardian 9/3/04

Teacher activity 2.2

Show students 15 minutes of a video/DVD. Ask them to take notes on a topic from the programme. Then divide the class into small groups and ask them to compare their notes and produce one set of notes for the group. As a whole class, discuss the strengths and shortcomings of the notes produced.

Teacher activity 2.3

Produce a set of cards showing common abbreviations such as *i.e.* and *e.g.*, and Economics abbreviations such as *PED* and *GDP*. Make a second set of cards with explanations of the abbreviations. Ask students, in groups, to match these.

Numeracy

At this level the key numerical skills are:
- calculating percentages;
- calculating percentage changes;
- calculating averages;
- interpreting index numbers;
- interpreting statistical tables;
- distinguishing between changes in growth rates and absolute changes.

You may find that your students have very different levels of mathematical competence. Even some of those with reasonable levels of numeracy may find numerical work rather off-putting. It is important to try to put them at their ease and to make them confident in undertaking numerical calculations. Confidence is the key to numerical competence, and this is gained through practice.

Some of the calculations that students will have to undertake are ones they are likely to be already familiar with. For example, in calculating total revenue, students have to multiply price by quantity, in calculating average cost they have to divide total cost by output, and in calculating profit they have to deduct costs from revenue.

Some students may be familiar with calculating percentages and percentage changes. As these are important calculations, it is worth checking early on in the course that all students are able to do them.

Of the three main ways of calculating the average, the most important one for Economics students is the **arithmetic mean**. This is relatively straightforward to calculate (total divided by the number of units). In coursework students may also make use of the **median** (the middle value of a series of figures) and the **mode** (the number occurring most frequently).

Understanding how index numbers are constructed will strengthen their ability to calculate and interpret index numbers in an Economics context. It also gives them the option of using index numbers in coursework.

Time should also be devoted to exploring the difference between changes in growth rates and absolute changes. Students can be asked, for instance, to interpret time series or tables showing economic growth rates or inflation rates.

Student activity 2.2

In groups or individually students could be asked to do the following:

- Calculate what percentage of the class is studying mathematics.
- From local newspaper advertisements, calculate the average price of houses or the average rent in the local area. This average can be tracked and compared over time.
- Convert national output figures into an index and work out annual percentage changes (economic growth).
- Calculate the cost of a basket of shopping in the local area on one day, and a month later calculate the cost of the same basket.
- Select four items – for example food, clothing, travel and books – and ask class members how much they spend a month on these items. Total the amounts and work out what proportion is spent on each item.

Teacher activity 2.4

Consider the strategy you would adopt in each of the following cases:

- a student finding it difficult to calculate price elasticity of demand;
- some members of the class do not understand the differences between percentage changes and changes in percentage points;
- a student interprets a fall in the inflation rate from 12 per cent to 8 per cent as a fall in prices;
- students are confused over the meaning of index number figures.

Interpreting data

Economists spend much of their time interpreting data. It is a skill which enables economists to evaluate economic theories, to examine economic trends and to assess the effects of economic policies. Its importance is reflected in examinations. It is tested in multiple-choice papers, in coursework and in structured questions papers. In such papers the data may come in a variety of forms, including newspaper articles, extracts from books and reports, statistical data and diagrams.

When answering questions based on given data, there are a number of key points of advice for students:

- Check the date and source of the data.
- Read through the questions first so that you know what you are looking for in the data.
- Check the data carefully. Take note of any general heading, headings of a table, footnotes and axes of diagrams. For instance, check whether statistical data is given in real or nominal figures.
- You might want to highlight key sentences.
- Check carefully whether figures are showing absolute changes or percentage changes.
- Go back and check the marks allocated to each question as this will give you an indication of the time you should devote to each one.
- You can answer the questions in any order, but it is advisable to answer them in the order in which they are set. This is to avoid overlap in your answers. It is also because the questions will have been set in a logical order and answering one question may help you answer the next question.
- Make use of both the data and your knowledge and understanding of Economics in answering the question.
- Make sure that what you write is clear and relevant.
- If appropriate, include diagrams in your answer.

Problem-solving

Much of Economics is about problem-solving. A good economist is one who can analyse the causes of a problem – for example, unemployment, pollution or world poverty – examine the consequences and make reasoned judgements about possible solutions.

Economics students need to consider different viewpoints and to base their decisions on economic analysis. Many students initially base their judgements on their own experience only and think in terms of one right answer to a problem, expecting the teacher to provide that 'answer'. They should be encouraged to distinguish between evidence and opinion, and to appreciate that the real world is a complex and ever-changing place, that economic theory is subject to limitations, and that there is often no 'right answer'.

Student activity 2.3

After having studied the topics, students could be asked to:

- give a presentation, perhaps in pairs, on the causes of population change in the country;
- consider what factors will determine whether allowing a foreign chemical company to set up in the country would provide a net benefit.

Diagrams

Diagrams play a vital role in Economics. They are used, for example, to illustrate changes in economic variables over time, to analyse changes in variables, and to assess the nature of economic relationships. It has been said that a picture is worth a thousand words. The same applies to diagrams.

Students need to be able to plot and draw diagrams, particularly demand and supply diagrams, and to interpret a range of diagrams. They should be required to use and comment on diagrams from the start of the course. This will increase their confidence and the accuracy of their work.

Drawing diagrams

Students should be encouraged to:

- produce clear diagrams – approximately a third of a page in size;
- use a ruler to draw the axes;
- label the axes accurately;
- label the curves accurately;
- explain what the diagram is showing.

Student activity 2.4

Each of the following diagrams contains a mistake, an omission, or a mistake and an omission. Make the necessary corrections and additions.

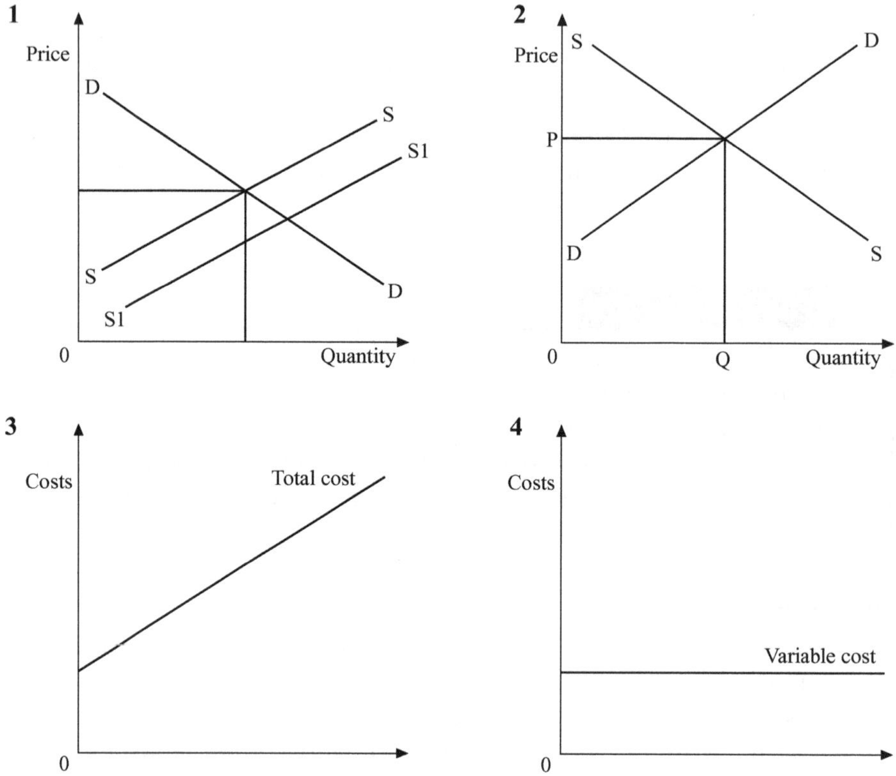

Figure 2.2: Common economics diagrams

Interpreting and using diagrams

Students should be familiar with a range of diagrams, including graphs showing the relationships between variables, pictograms, pie charts, bar charts, time series graphs and cartograms.

Graphs showing the relationships between variables

An example is demand and price. Students need to recognise whether the graphs show a positive or a negative relationship. They should check what the axes represent, the scales, and whether the value of one variable rises or falls in response to a change in the other variable. Care has to be taken in interpreting graphs. A graph illustrates a possible relationship but does not itself prove or explain that relationship.

Pictograms

These use pictures or symbols to show data. For example, a pinman could be used to represent 100,000 unemployed, as shown in Figure 2.3. A key has to be provided with a pictogram, indicating the quantity represented by each picture. Pictograms have the advantage that they can present data in a simple and clear manner and so can be useful in coursework. However, it may not be possible for a symbol to represent a low value since they may involve the use of too many pictures or symbols in some diagrams.

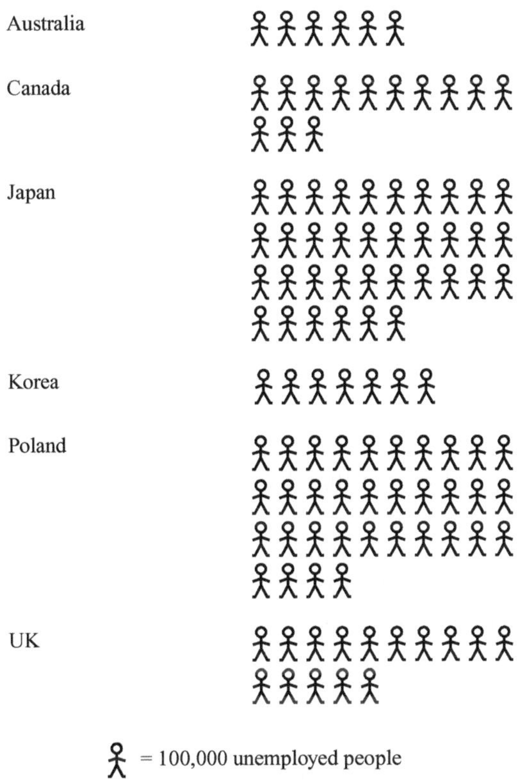

Figure 2.3: Unemployment in 2004 in selected countries

Pie charts

The name is derived from the fact that these circular diagrams are divided into slices. These are designed to be easy to interpret. They usually show the percentage values of the components of a total; for instance, the percentage contribution of particular taxes to total tax revenue.

When showing percentages, the percentage has to be multiplied by 3.6 (since total percentage = 100, whilst the total value of degrees = 360). So, for example, 40 per cent would be converted to 40 × 3.6 = 144 degrees. If actual figures are used, they should be expressed as a fraction of the total and then multiplied by 360. For example, rent of $60 out of a total cost of $300 would be converted to $60 ÷ $300 × 360 = 72 degrees.

Bar charts

These consist of one or more bars (columns), in which the length of the bar indicates the magnitude of the data. They are used to show a comparison of the size of the quantities of similar items. The bars can be drawn vertically or horizontally. They can also be drawn with or without a gap between them. Bar charts are quite often used in multiple-choice papers.

Time series graph

This is the name given to a series of figures recorded over time. The series may be plotted at daily, weekly, monthly, yearly or another interval of time, and the horizontal axis (the *x* axis) is always chosen as the time axis. Students should be taught how to read a trend from a time series graph.

Cartogram

This is a way of presenting geographical data. It involves drawing a map to show, for example, unemployment percentage by area. Shading can be used, with a key or figures placed on the map. It involves more preparation than some diagrams since a map has to be drawn or reproduced and divided into the desired regions. Nevertheless, it can be a clear and attractive way to display information and can be used in coursework.

Teacher activity 2.5

Ask students to present Economics information in a variety of forms. For example, students could be asked to compare a range of countries' economic growth rates on a bar chart, the country's inflation rate over the last ten years on a time series graph, regional income levels on a cartogram, share of different forms of government spending in total government expenditure on a pie chart, and the population of a number of countries on a pictogram. The best work could be displayed on the classroom wall.

Student activity 2.5

1 Decide which would be the best form of diagram to illustrate:

a) the relationship between the supply of labour and the wage rate;

b) the current account position of a country over the last five years;

c) unemployment rates in different countries.

2 Explain what the following diagrams show.

1

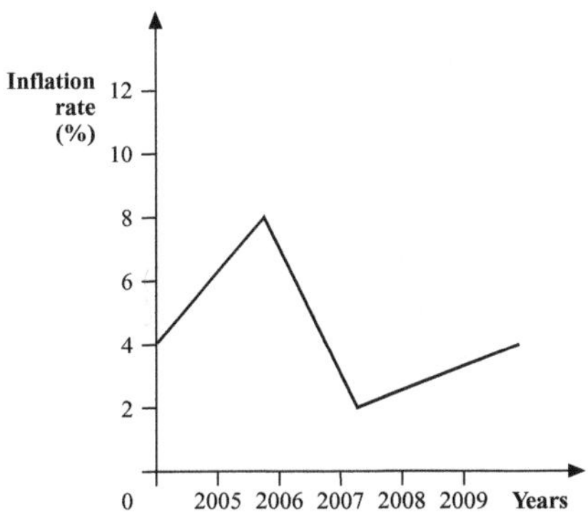

2

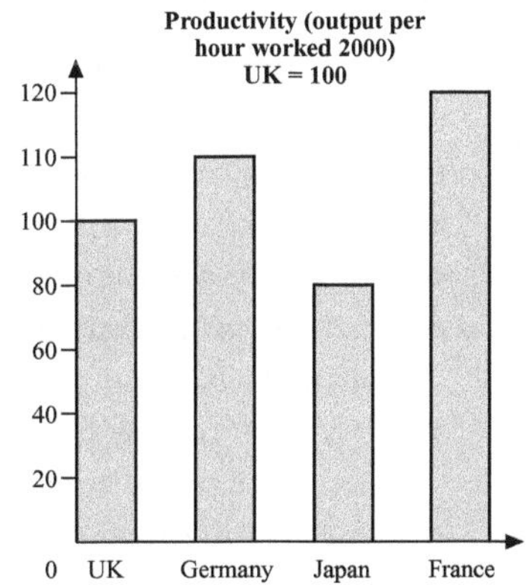

3

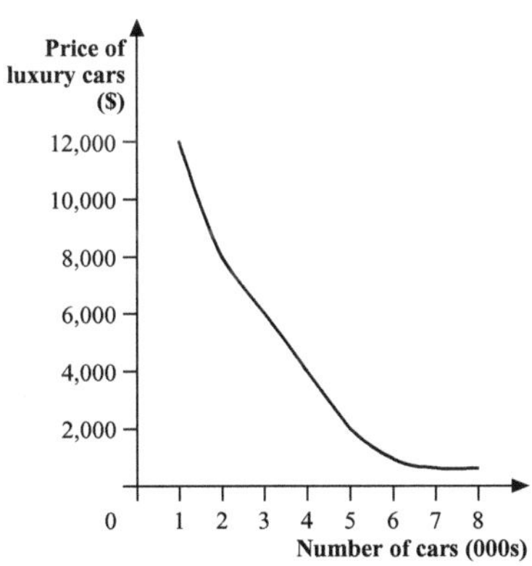

Figure 2.4: Interpreting diagrams

ICT skills

ICT is becoming increasingly important for students of all subjects. Encouraging students to develop their ICT skills will enhance their learning in Economics in a number of ways. These include increasing their access to information, enabling them to undertake investigations, and improving the presentation of their work. Students can also undertake learning activities and assess and model economic performance and decisions by using relevant websites.

LOOKING BACK

This chapter has emphasised the need for Economics students to develop a range of skills. In reviewing this chapter you might want to consider the following:

- Do you stretch all of your students' oral skills sufficiently?
- Are there opportunities for you to use simulation exercises?
- How do you address the problem of students taking different amounts of time to complete worksheets?
- How can you best integrate the development of numerical skills into your teaching?
- Do you encourage your students to recognise the limitations of Economics data?
- How is data interpretation linked to other skills?
- Do you make sufficient use of diagrams throughout the course?
- How could the use of ICT enhance your students' skills?

3 Interpreting the syllabus

The course that you plan for your students will clearly be informed by the syllabus. An introductory syllabus, such as the CIE IGCSE, is based on students having no prior knowledge of Economics. You should bear this in mind and expect to proceed relatively slowly at first.

Economics is a developmental subject. Terms and concepts introduced in one topic are then used in other topics. This means that students' understanding builds up progressively. For many students there is often a Eureka moment when the subject suddenly clicks and they start to think like an economist. This may come towards the end of covering the content of the course. For this reason I like to leave a reasonable amount of time to recap the topics, examine the links between them, and engage in class revision.

You need to build in some flexibility to allow for students finding some topics and activities more difficult than you expected.

Factors to bear in mind when drawing up a scheme of work

There are a number of factors you should consider when planning how you are going to deliver the syllabus. These include:

- the time available to you;
- the skills you need to develop;
- the need to relate the subject to real-world examples;
- the learning activities you could use;
- the abilities and interests of you and your students.

Micro versus macro

There is some debate amongst Economics teachers as to whether it is better to teach micro-topics or macro-topics first. I have done both, but have found, like many teachers, that starting with micro-topics works much better. I think this is because it is initially easier to relate micro-topics to students' own experiences, to make the links between topics, and to develop skills in this way.

Most syllabuses adopt this approach. Indeed as most are logical and well thought out, it often pays to follow the sequence of the syllabus.

Further information on the syllabus

There are a number of ways in which you can get more insight into the syllabus and how to develop it. Past examination papers, mark schemes, examiners' reports and inset sessions provide information on the depth and approach that the examination board is expecting. Discussions with other teachers following the same syllabus are likely to prove particularly fruitful.

Teacher activity 3.1

Collect past examination papers, mark schemes and examiners' reports and assess how much time you should devote to the first topic of the syllabus.

Key features of a syllabus

The syllabus is the most important document for teachers. It provides the crucial information on which you need to base your scheme of work.

The important components of a syllabus include these:

- The aims of the syllabus. It would be useful to discuss these with students at the start of the course.
- Assessment objectives and their weightings. For the IGCSE examination these are knowledge and understanding, judgement and decision-making, and investigation.
- The scheme of assessment. This section describes the examination papers, gives their weightings and time length, and informs you of the combination of papers candidates can sit.
- Curriculum content. This gives details of the topics to be covered.
- Coursework details. These include the range of topics from which centres can select, assessment criteria, moderation procedure and grade descriptions.

Converting the syllabus into a programme of study

Having studied the syllabus, you can plan your scheme of work. This should ensure that not only do you cover the subject matter, but also that you enable students to develop the necessary skills and that you evaluate that learning at regular intervals.

In drawing up your scheme of work, you may find it useful to use a matrix style that provides information:

Content	Assessment objectives	Learning activities	Resources	No. of lessons / Timing	Evaluation / Revision of the lesson

Such an approach could be used for each part of a topic, but it is important to bear in mind the need to encourage students to see the connections between topics.

Teacher activity 3.2

Draw up, for students, an outline of what you plan to cover each week.

Suggested approach to planning lessons on demand, supply and price determination

Start by looking back to the Economics problem and the role of the price mechanism in a market economy. Then you could use a case study on the change in price of a particular product familiar to students. This could be, for example, computers, trainers, football shirts or newspapers/magazines. The case study could be based on newspaper articles, should use non-technical language, and should bring out, in general terms, why the price has changed – for example the product becoming more popular or cheaper to produce.

After this, the students could be asked to carry out a survey in the class on what quantities of a given soft drink they would buy at different prices. You could discuss their findings and get the students to plot the information on a demand diagram.

Having established the relationship between price and demand, you could go on to consider some of the factors that would cause a shift in the demand curve – including change in income, change in price of related products, and advertising. You could do this in a variety of ways, including:

- worksheets based on real-world examples;
- products described are complements or substitutes;
- a video on advertising;
- exercises from a textbook.

Then your focus could turn to supply. You might be able to invite a local producer or retailer to talk about how they react to price changes and what factors would cause them to increase or decrease their supply.

Again, there is a range of ways in which you could explore movements along and shifts in the supply curve. In addition to worksheets and exercises from a textbook, you might want to consider using the following:

- Cards with brief descriptions of events affecting a particular product (e.g. the impact of advances in technology on mobile phones) which students have to match with cards stating contraction in supply, extension in supply, increase in supply and decrease in supply.
- Group work discussing the factors affecting the supply of a particular product, followed by reporting back to the whole class.

Having covered demand and supply, you could move back to price determination and changes in price. In explaining price determination, it is important to cover why price moves towards the equilibrium. You could look at examples of shortages and surpluses. When examining the effects of changes in demand and supply, it is helpful to use case studies. Candidates should be required to draw a number of demand and supply diagrams and to explain what they are showing. You could ask students to draw some diagrams for wall displays. Then you could recap the topic in a number of ways, including:

- multiple-choice questions;
- structured questions.

Suggested approach to planning introductory lessons on the main aims of government policy

You could introduce this topic by showing students different political parties' manifestos or government statements – bringing out differences in their economic aims and policies. You could also invite two or three middle-aged local people to talk about their experiences of changes in living standards, inflation and employment opportunities over time. Then you could provide simple statistical information on unemployment, inflation, balance of payments deficit and economic growth in your home country and three other major economies, and ask students in groups to decide which economy is performing best.

Teacher activity 3.3

Consider how you might approach teaching costs of production and what learning activities you could employ.

LOOKING BACK

Careful planning of the delivery of the course should make your teaching easy and more enjoyable, and should improve the performance of your students. Look back to some of the issues covered in this chapter and ask yourself these questions:

- Are you fully familiar with all aspects of the syllabus?
- Do you devote enough time and attention to planning your lessons?
- Can you see ways in which you could organise your teaching more effectively?

4 Teaching strategies

There are various ways of promoting learning and of assessing the quality of that learning. The teaching strategies adopted to promote learning are influenced by a number of factors, including institutional policy, ability range of students, topics covered, teacher preference and availability of resources.

In the vast majority of cases, however, the most effective teaching approach is one that promotes active learning and that integrates assessment with the learning process.

A variety of teaching strategies should make learning more interesting and should enable students with differing strengths to gain a sense of achievement. The assignments set and assessment conducted should be part of the learning process.

Student activity 4.1

- Ask students to consider which of the following types of learning styles best describes their own:
  - enthusiastic: likes variety and enjoys undertaking new work;
  - imaginative: has ideas on new ways of tackling work and sees connections between topics;
  - practical: works well with not much guidance and good at setting goals;
  - logical: tackles work in an organised way and enjoys problem-solving.
- Ask students to identify strengths and weaknesses of each style:
  - enthusiastic: willing to ask for assistance and works well in groups, but not good at organisation and tends to leave things to the last minute;
  - imaginative: willing to share ideas and good at coming up with new solutions to problems, but may be easily distracted and may overlook important detail;

– practical: well organised and gets things done on time, but may get bogged down with details and does not always work well with others;
– logical: thorough and plans well in advance, but may spend too much time on organising information and may be over-cautious.

Differentiation

Students who opt to study Economics are often among the more able but, nevertheless, any class is likely to include students with a mixed range of abilities. As well as differences in interest and motivation, students are likely to have differences in their ability to:

- concentrate;
- carry out numerical tasks;
- read;
- communicate in a written form;
- communicate orally;
- grasp new concepts;
- apply theories to real-world examples;
- analyse;
- evaluate.

It is obviously important to involve all students and to stretch the abilities of every member of the class. A teaching approach which takes into account the current abilities, needs and potential of individual students is known as **differentiation**.

Differentiation can be achieved in a number of ways. One is by using a variety of active learning strategies. This variation should increase students' concentration and raise their performance. Students who are not very good at, for example, using a computer may do well in role-playing exercises. Also, within any particular activity, students of different abilities can be asked to complete different tasks or a different number of tasks. Some resources can be geared to different levels of ability and students can be allowed to develop skills at different rates.

Allowing students of different abilities to interact can benefit all. The more able students will have their understanding tested and will develop their ability to communicate. The less able students will hear explanations expressed in language they are likely to understand, and are likely to be stimulated by the ideas of the more able. The need to make learning both accessible and challenging to all members of the group should be taken into account when undertaking group work. On some occasions you may wish to have mixed-ability groups with individual members being given different tasks. On other occasions you may want to have groups composed of students with similar abilities working on the same task.

Adopting a teaching style which takes into account the different abilities of students can initially be quite demanding and time consuming. It should, however, generate greater interest in your lessons and better examination performance, and may even save you time in the long run.

Didactic teaching

A formal presentation by the teacher may form part of some lessons, but it is advisable to avoid over-reliance on this approach. You may want to introduce a topic, on occasions, by giving a brief, formal talk.

You may also sometimes need to dictate notes to impart some brief updates. However, it is crucial to limit or avoid using dictated notes. I have seen some lessons that have consisted entirely of the teacher reading out notes and students trying to write down every word. In such a situation, all the students are learning is how to write quickly. They are not thinking about what they are writing. Indeed, they could be writing about anything. The process keeps the students quiet, but it is boring and unproductive and does not provide any opportunity for differentiation.

Active learning

Active learning involves students thinking, participating fully and taking some responsibility for their own learning. Instead of students being passive recipients of information, they become active learners.

There are various ways of promoting active learning, including:

- question-and-answer sessions;
- brainstorming;
- flow diagrams;
- worksheets;
- discussions;
- role playing and simulations;
- outside speakers;
- visits;
- wall displays;
- case studies;
- presentations;
- producing a newspaper;
- ICT activities.

Question-and-answer sessions

This is a relatively simple, straightforward, but potentially very productive teaching strategy. Short question-and-answer sessions keep students alert and enable you to assess their progress. Some students, however, may be less confident and/or less able to answer oral questions. Account should be taken of this. Initially, questions requiring short or more straightforward answers might be directed to such students.

Students can be questioned not only about what has been covered in class but also about, for example, recent economic events, how they could approach examination questions, and other activities such as visits.

Some of the questions should be closed questions in the sense that you are expecting certain answers. Others, however, should be open questions with a variety of potential answers.

As well as oral answers, you can ask students to illustrate points on the board. For example, a student could be asked to explain by drawing a diagram what will happen to the price of sugar if a subsidy is placed on sugar.

Student activity 4.2

Individual students or pairs of students could be given a strip of paper with a key Economics term written on it – for example, *unemployment, price elasticity of demand, saving and money*. They could then be asked to illustrate the term on the board without using letters and without speaking. The other members of the class have to decide what the term is.

Brainstorming

Brainstorming can be used in a number of situations. For example, students could be asked for their views on what influences how much people save and what factors indicate a high standard of living. Their ideas could be written up on the board or a flipchart, and the class could then discuss their significance. Brainstorming has a number of advantages, including that it:

- encourages independent thinking;
- can show that students' ideas are valued;
- enables the whole group to be involved.

Flow diagrams

Flow diagrams are useful in Economics as they encourage students to think through the sequence of events and to see the links between causes and consequences. You could draw examples on the board:

1

Fall in demand

↓

Demand curve shifts to the left

↓

Price falls

↓

Supply contracts

2

Fall in income tax rates

↓

Rise in disposable income

↓

Rise in demand

↓

Rise in employment

You could then ask students to fill in the gaps in other flow diagrams and to construct some of their own.

Worksheets

Although worksheets take time to prepare, they do have a number of advantages. They can:

- with updating, be used for a number of years;
- break down the subject into manageable steps;
- be used in combination with a textbook;
- be based on local examples;
- enable students who have missed lessons to catch up;
- be used for revision and test purposes.

They also allow for differentiation. A different worksheet can be given to some students, and/or students can be required to answer a different number of questions. Worksheets can be based on a piece of prose, a set of figures, diagrams or a mixture of all three. In designing worksheets, it is important to make them look as attractive and professional as possible.

Do not try to put too much on a page. It is important that the language is pitched at the right level. The first questions set should be the most straightforward, with the level of difficulty increasing towards the last question.

Discussions

Economics is a subject of ideas and controversies in which discussion plays a key part.

The quality of students' discussions increases with their maturity, their grasp of the subject and their experience of participating in discussions. At first, it may be useful to have general discussions based on your students' experiences, applying these to relevant economic concepts and events through careful questioning. As the course progresses, students' ability to make use of Economics concepts and current events should increase without prompting.

Discussion can occur on a number of levels. As well as a whole-class discussion, you can have small-group discussions and discussions between pairs of students. In each case it is useful to have some ground rules – including that people's views are to be treated with respect – and to have a purpose for the discussion.

A whole-class discussion could be held, for instance, on the relative merits of different economic systems, with students being asked after the discussion to write up the general points advanced. You might also set up a debate, with two or three students being asked to speak for free trade and two or three speaking in favour of protectionism. The rest of the group could then vote on the basis of the strengths of the arguments advanced.

In small groups, students could be asked to discuss why some countries have different income levels, and then report back to the whole class. Allowing students to discuss topics will increase their knowledge and understanding. It is easy to think that a student has understood something; a true test of this is whether they can explain it to someone else.

Role playing and simulations

Role playing and simulations can help to involve the whole class, develop a range of skills and enable students of different abilities to achieve. For example, the class could be divided into groups representing multinational companies, trade unions, government, local residents and environmental groups to investigate whether a chemical company should be built in the area. Students should be given briefing sheets to study before the exercise.

If successful, the same exercise might be used again, with members of the class undertaking different roles. Students could then be asked to discuss what extra insights they have gained from seeing the issue from a different viewpoint.

It is useful to keep the exercise focused on one major issue. Roles can be allocated according to both ability and confidence in undertaking such an activity. Less able students can be given less demanding roles, and less confident students can be given roles which require less active roles – for example, minute takers and observers.

At the end of a role-playing or simulation exercise, students can discuss and then write down the key points that have been brought out by the exercise.

Outside speakers

On a few occasions, one or two local people could be invited to a class to talk to your students and then answer questions. For example, a person could be asked about their experiences of inflation or unemployment, choice of occupation, or what it is like to work for the government.

Such talks can make a topic come alive for students. The people invited can provide real-world examples, up-to-date information and different perspectives. They may, however, not have much experience of speaking to a group of young people. It may therefore be useful to discuss with them how to approach the talk. It is advisable to ask them to keep the talk relatively brief and to devote more time to a question-and-answer session at the end.

Visits

Visits, even half-day visits, can generate extra interest in the subject and can enable students to see the relevance of economic theory and to apply theories.

Some students will remember a visit for a long time, and an enjoyable visit can help to build good relationships in the group. A visit also enables students to see Economics in action and to relate economic theory to the real world.

To get full value from a visit, it is important to integrate it into your teaching programme, fitting it in with the preceding and succeeding lessons. The topic or topics involved in the visit should be explored with students beforehand. The purpose of the visit should be discussed and students should be provided with notebooks in which to write the answers to questions and other findings. Afterwards students in groups could be asked to write a report on the visit or to give a presentation on it.

It is crucial to plan a visit carefully. Planning should involve a number of stages:

- determining the objectives of the visit;
- seeking permission for the visit;
- discussing the focus and organisation of the visit with those involved;
- obtaining information on the visit;
- arranging transport;
- preparing briefing notes for the students.

There is a range of visits that could be undertaken. For instance, a visit could be made to a local firm to investigate the features of a particular type of business organisation, changes in costs and output policies. A visit could be made to a local dockyard to consider questions relating to international trade, or to a local market to consider questions of scarcity and price determination.

Wall displays

Students can be given responsibility for wall displays. Different students could be assigned to different displays. These could include definitions of key terms, price elasticity of demand (PED) calculations, photographs and details of visits, newspaper cuttings, and mini-biographies of famous economists. It is useful to get these displays laminated if possible, as they will then appear more professional and will last longer.

Using wall displays makes a classroom look more attractive and can give students a sense of ownership of the room. It also generates interest in the subject among younger students who may be deciding what subjects to study.

Case studies

A number of key Economics concepts can be explored by using problem-solving case studies. Such an approach develops students' skills of application, analysis and evaluation, and can make the subject seem more relevant.

Scarcity, choice, opportunity cost, social costs and benefits could be examined by asking small groups of students to decide on how a piece of local land should be used.

Students could be provided with data on a firm, real or hypothetical. Then, in groups again, students could be asked to consider how the firm might raise its revenue. This would enable them to consider the significance of demand, costs, revenue and advertising.

They could also explore how a recent event – for example, the Olympic games in Athens – may have affected a country's balance of payments, employment and gross domestic product (GDP). They could be given, for instance, photographs of people arriving in the country and of spectators at events, newspaper articles and videos.

It is important when using a case study produced by someone else or in preparing one yourself to ensure that the information is generally representative and not atypical.

Teacher activity 4.1

Consider what information you would need to give students for a case study on changes in the price of oil and what Economics concepts it could be used to examine.

Presentations

Presentations can be given to the class, other members of the school, or invited outside groups such as parents or members of a firm the group has visited. They can be combined with a number of other activities. A presentation can be given on not only the findings of a visit, but also on decisions recorded in case studies, on individual or group investigations into particular topics, and current economic events. Depending on availability, ICT can be used in presentations – from overhead projectors to PowerPoint.

Students should be given careful guidance on how to give presentations. Nevertheless, they are likely to find the prospect rather daunting. For this reason, it can be useful to ask students to make presentations in groups of two or three.

There is a potential problem with group presentations – the contribution of the members of the group may vary. The problem can be overcome, to some extent, by requiring each member of the group to provide a separate written report, including an assessment of how the presentation process was completed.

Producing a newspaper

You could get the students to produce a short school newspaper which could be distributed to other students. Ideas for articles could be gained by examining national newspapers and economics magazines, watching local news programmes and interviewing local people. Having discussed the ideas, the class could be divided into groups to produce articles on, for example, a new firm setting up in the area, a local strike, and changes in house prices. Students could also produce an economics crossword and report on successes of past Economics students.

ICT activities

ICT activities can enhance the quality of students' work and add variety to lessons. Most students now expect to use ICT in their study.

There are a number of factors that influence the ICT activities that you set your students. These include the following:

- The time available. Normally time is limited, and it is important that the activities are relatively short and focused so that the use of ICT does enhance learning.
- The amount of ICT skills your students have. I find that most of my students possess better ICT skills than I do. If, however, students lack basic ICT skills, you will need to give them some introductory advice. You could have students working in twos and threes, with students with strong ICT skills helping those with less experience.
- The ICT equipment available to you and your students. You may have computers in your classroom or you may have to book a computer room. You may have access to a computer per student or you may have fewer computers than students.
- What to do if there are technical problems. You need to have a back-up strategy.
- The need to check an activity thoroughly beforehand. Assess the skills and time that will be required to complete it, and make sure that the information is available and the language accessible. Also remember that website addresses can change.

Teacher activity 4.2

Taking into account the factors listed above, prepare an ICT activity requiring students to produce a report and/or give a presentation on the difference in economic performance between two countries.

Developing assignments

Assignments are set to enable students to apply their knowledge and understanding and to develop their skills, and also to give them practice at answering examination questions and to provide them with feedback on their performance and suggestions for improvement.

Understanding of Economics concepts and skills builds up progressively. Assignments should reflect this. The first assignments set might be based on short questions and/or multiple-choice questions on a narrow range of topics. As the course progresses, assignments should involve some longer questions; cover a variety of topics; and assess not only knowledge and understanding, but also analysis, judgement and decision-making. In addition you can build up the use of past examination questions.

For some assignments you may want to give some extra, rather more searching questions to the more able students.

I find it useful to establish a clear pattern of homework at the start of the course. I set the homework on the same day each week, give the students one week to complete it, and tell them to return it on a fixed day each week.

Assessment

There is both formative and summative assessment. **Formative assessment** occurs throughout the course. This type of assessment can take a variety of forms, including questions, observing, marking of classwork and homework, tests, student self-assessment and mid-term reports.

The aims of formative assessment are to monitor progress, to provide regular feedback to students, to produce information on which to plan targets and teaching strategies, and thereby to improve student performance.

Summative assessment reviews what progress has been made at particular intervals and at the end of the course. The main forms of summative assessment are end-of-topic tests, assessment of completed coursework, examinations and end-of-course reports.

Such assessment provides information to students, parents, employers and the school about the level that the students have reached.

To be effective, it is important to make clear to students what standard they are expected to reach, how to check their progress, and how they will be assessed by you and in the examination. Involve them in the assessment process. At the start of the course you should give students a copy of the syllabus. They could keep this at the front of their files and refer to it as they cover the topics. Partway through the course you could show and discuss with them mark schemes and reports produced by the examination board.

It is important when marking classwork and homework that you explain to students what the marks or grades you give them mean. For example, what does 15 out of 20 indicate? Does an A grade suggest that the student is expected to progress to an A grade in the examination, or have they already reached that standard? You should relate marks and grades to skill levels, providing positive comments and useful suggestions for future improvement.

The more you can get your students to review their own performance, reflect on their own strengths and weakness, and draw up action plans,

Example of student questionnaire (see page 38)

For student use		**For staff use**	
Do you believe you are making progress in this subject?		Do you believe the student is making progress?	
Yes	No	Yes	No
If you ticked No, please try to explain why you are not making progress.		If you ticked No, explain why you believe the student is not making progress.	
Do you find it easy to concentrate in class?		Are you satisfied with the student's concentration in class?	
Yes	No	Yes	No
Please give reasons.		Comments	
Are you devoting sufficient time and effort to the the homework set?		Are you satisfied with the student's work effort on homework set?	
Yes	No	Yes	No
If you have ticked No, give reasons		Comments	
What strengths do you have in this subject?		Comments	
Which skills do you find it most difficult to master?		Recommendations	
What do you like about the subject?		Comments	
What do you dislike about the subject?		Comments	

the more progress they are likely to make. This self-assessment can occur in a number of ways, including in discussion and in the reporting process. The form on page 37 is an example of getting first the student and then you to reflect on their progress. The intention would be for you to discuss the comments with your students.

You may also wish to involve students in assessing the group-learning process by asking them to fill in a questionnaire. I tend to find students' comments very useful and have adjusted my teaching as a result. Below are some of the questions you might want to consider including in a student questionnaire:

- Do you enjoy lessons?
- Is there enough variety in lessons?
- Which activities do you learn most from?
- Do you feel comfortable asking questions in class?
- Are diagrams drawn on the board clear?
- Is the amount of homework set too much, about right or too little?
- Do you have any problems understanding the questions set?
- Which resources do you use when undertaking assignments?
- Do you find the comments written on your homework useful?

LOOKING BACK

Using a variety of teaching strategies that encourage active learning and appropriate assessment strategies should keep your students interested, motivated and on course for good grades. This chapter has offered you some ideas. You may wish to reflect on the following questions:

- ◆ Are your students clear about the objectives of your lessons?
- ◆ Do your students enjoy and learn from your lessons?
- ◆ Are you using a variety of teaching strategies?
- ◆ Do your lessons help in developing a variety of skills, or is there a tendency to concentrate on only one?
- ◆ Are your students able to apply concepts and analyse real-world events?
- ◆ Do you give students of all abilities a sense of achievement?
- ◆ Do you provide your students with opportunities for self-assessment?

5 Multiple-choice questions

Introduction

Most examination boards require students to sit a multiple-choice question paper consisting of 40 questions. To do well in this paper students need to develop both a good grasp of Economics and a good multiple-choice technique.

Through hard work and careful preparation, students should be able to perform well in multiple-choice papers and gain high marks.

The nature of multiple-choice questions

Multiple-choice questions start with a stem. This is either a question or an incomplete statement. The stem of some of the questions is based on a diagram or some real-world data.

Following the stem are four options labelled A to D. The correct option is called the **key**. The other, incorrect, options are known as **distractors**.

Example 5.1: Multiple-choice questions

In 2003 the GDP of Jordan increased in real terms at an annual rate of 1 per cent and its population rose by 4 per cent. In the same year Vietnam's real GDP rose at an annual rate of 6 per cent and its population grew by 3 per cent.

What conclusion may be drawn from this statement?

A Real GDP per head rose in Vietnam but fell in Jordan.
B The real GDP of Vietnam was higher than that of Jordan.
C The standard of living was higher in Vietnam.
D Vietnam experienced a higher rate of inflation.

Teacher activity 5.1

- Obtain copies of past multiple-choice papers from your examination board.
- Provide your students with plenty of opportunity to work through these questions.

Skills tested

The skills tested by multiple-choice questions can be grouped in a number of ways. One grouping is into those assessing knowledge and understanding and those assessing analysis. Sixty per cent of questions (i.e. 24 questions) in the IGCSE multiple-choice paper test knowledge and understanding of facts, definitions, concepts, principles and theories, Economics vocabulary, terminology and conventions.

The remaining 40 per cent of questions (i.e. 16 questions) test analysis. This is a higher-order skill. It requires candidates to select, organise and interpret data; apply economic data; recognise patterns in such data and deduce relationships.

The skills tested can also be grouped in terms of the ability to interpret written information, tables and diagrams, and the ability to undertake numerical calculations. The written information may be in the form of a short question or a more detailed scenario with a question. Some questions are based on advertisements.

There are likely to be four or five questions based on tables. These may be on a range of topics including demand and supply, costs of production, and indicators of development and trade position. Sometimes there is information in the tables that is not relevant to the question. This is deliberate; as noted above, one of the skills that examiners are seeking to test is the ability to select and use relevant data.

Diagrams take a number of forms. The most common are demand and supply graphs and cost and revenue graphs. Papers often include two or three time series graphs. There may also be questions based on bar charts and pie charts.

Questions that test numerical skills include those asking students to calculate PED and working out average cost.

Increasingly, questions of all sorts are based on real-world data.

Teacher activity 5.2

Read the reports on past examinations published by your examination board. The ones from CIE, for example, are very informative. They emphasise the importance of candidates recognising the difference between percentage and absolute changes, understanding the meaning of real figures and avoiding confusing a slower growth rate with an absolute decline.

Student activity 5.1

Whilst covering a topic, ask students to undertake tasks that develop a range of skills. For instance, when studying inflation students could answer these questions:

1 Define inflation. (Knowledge and understanding)

2 Study the data below and explain what happened to the general price level in the United States between 2000 and 2002. (Interpretation of tabular information)

Year	Inflation rate (%)
2000	2.5
2001	2.0
2002	1.4

3 Represent the current weightings in your country's consumer price index in a pie chart. (Use of diagrams)

4 A country's family expenditure survey finds that 20 per cent of its population's expenditure goes on food, 20 per cent on housing, 10 per cent on clothing, 25 per cent on entertainment and 25 per cent on transport. The price of food rises by 20 per cent, the price of housing increases by 5 per cent, the price of clothing falls by 10 per cent, the price of entertainment is unchanged, and the price of transport rises by 20 per cent. Calculate the change in the price level. (Numeracy)

5 In the early 2000s Zimbabwe experienced a high rate of cost-push inflation. This imposed a number of costs on Zimbabwean consumers and firms.

a) Distinguish between demand-pull and cost-push inflation.

b) Discuss the costs of inflation.

(Knowledge and understanding)

6 A government is considering what action to take to reduce the demand-pull inflation the country is experiencing. Identify two appropriate policy measures it could employ and explain how these might reduce inflation. (Analysis)

Coverage of multiple-choice examinations

Multiple-choice examinations have the advantage, from the examination board's point of view, that they test a wide area of the syllabus. The paper-setters try to ensure that the examination is well balanced, in terms both of the skills tested and the syllabus coverage.

> **Teacher activity 5.3**
>
> Check the examination reports to gain an awareness of the areas of the syllabus that are generally poorly answered. In recent years these have included international trade; the balance of payments; the meaning of profits; and the links between fixed and variable costs, revenue and profits.

Advice on answering multiple-choice questions

Multiple-choice questions should be an integral part of your teaching. At the beginning of the course give your students general advice on how to answer multiple-choice questions. Such advice should include these points:

- Read the questions very carefully. Do not rush.
- Consider the answer before looking at the options.
- Consider each option in turn.
- If you are finding a question particularly difficult, leave it and come back to it later.
- To answer some questions, it is useful to draw a diagram. This may help you work out the correct answer.
- Never leave a question unanswered. Even if you have no idea of the correct answer, you have a one-in-four chance of guessing the correct answer.

In addition, under test/examination conditions:

- fill in the answer sheet carefully;
- if you change your mind, rub out your original answer and mark in the new one carefully.

Using multiple-choice questions

Start your students answering multiple-choice questions early in the course. This will not only provide students with practice and confidence in answering this type of question, but it will also enable you and the students themselves to monitor their mastery of particular topics and their overall progress.

You can get students to work through a number of multiple-choice questions when you have completed a topic. For instance, after covering the basic economic problem section of the syllabus, you could set your students the task of completing approximately ten multiple-choice questions on the topic. These questions could be taken from the students' textbook or from past papers, or could be questions you have designed yourself.

You could tell students to complete the questions for homework, in a test or in class. In the last case you could ask students to answer the questions either on their own or in groups. Working in groups can be very productive in improving multiple-choice performance. This is because students know that they will have to think through their answers carefully as they will have to justify their choices to their colleagues.

In considering students' answers, it is worth analysing the thinking behind incorrect responses. For instance, you may find that a number of students are confusing a balance of payments deficit with a budget deficit. Time should be devoted in class to correcting such confusion.

Keep some past multiple-choice examination papers to use in class tests and mock examinations. Make sure you give students the same amount of time as they will have in the examination – for most examination boards approximately one-and-a-half minutes per question.

Teacher activity 5.4

Soon after the start of the course you could give students:

- ten relatively straightforward multiple-choice questions;
- a set of four different coloured cards (e.g. blue for A, red for B, green for C and yellow for D).

When they have completed the questions, you could ask them to hold up a card for each question.

Teacher activity 5.5

Ask students to study a multiple-choice question. Then ask them individually or in groups to:

- identify the concept/issue being tested;
- answer the question;
- explain why they think it is the correct option;
- explain why each of the other options is incorrect.

Teacher activity 5.6

One way in which students are becoming more familiar with multiple-choice questions is through television and radio quiz programmes. On some occasions you may want to ask the students to work on 10–15 multiple-choice questions in groups (teams). Then you could hold a quiz, giving marks for correct answers and for explanations. You may wish to build in some extra factors, for example:

- allowing each team to go 50:50 on one question of their choice (i.e. asking you to eliminate two wrong answers);
- permitting each team to ask your advice on one question;
- giving each team the opportunity to swap one question for an unseen question on the same topic.

Designing multiple-choice questions

Designing your own multiple-choice questions will provide more questions for use with your students and will help you understand how these questions are designed.

There are a number of ways of designing multiple-choice questions. The easiest is probably to adapt an existing examination question. For example, in the October/November 2002 paper, a question set asked: 'Which statement about fixed costs is correct?' This (and the options) could be adapted to 'Which statement about variable costs is correct?'

When designing questions from scratch, it is usually better for the stem to be in question form rather than sentence-completion form. Arrange the options in alphabetical order or, in the case of numerical options, in ascending or descending order of magnitude. Be careful to ensure that all the distractors are relatively strong and plausible. Try to avoid negative questions – for example, 'Which of the following is not a cause of inflation?'

Some of the questions you set should be based on diagrams and some should require students to undertake numerical calculations. It is particularly useful to use real-world data as the basis for a question. Articles from newspapers, Economics magazines, television news programmes and Internet sites are useful sources.

Whenever you come across a possible idea for a question, jot it down and then develop it when you have time. When you first set it for your students, assess how it performs. In particular, did students find it unambiguous and did it differentiate well?

Teacher activity 5.7

Use the following information as the basis for designing your own multiple-choice questions:

1 Which of the following is an example of the factor of production known as capital?

A a truck
B a truck driver
C a truck driver's savings
D a truck driver's wage.
(May/June 2001, Q1)

Adapt this question to one asking students to identify an example of labour from options based on nursing.

2

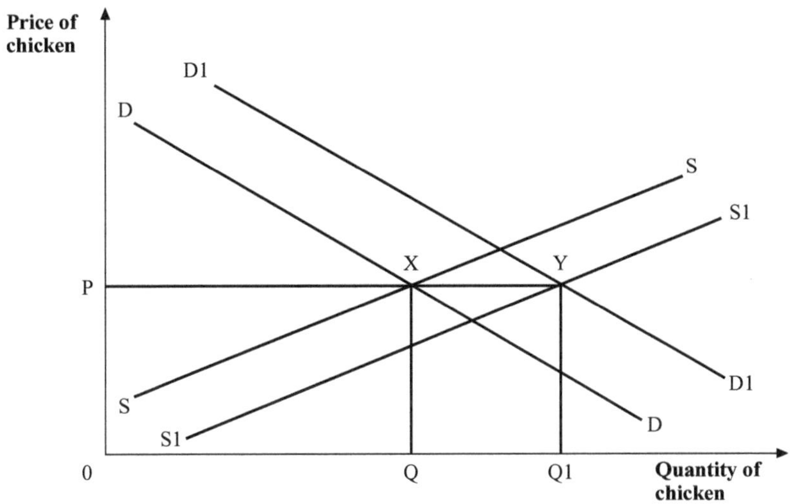

Ask students what could cause the equilibrium point to move from X to Y, and design a correct option and three other plausible options.

3 Select a macroeconomics problem and ask students which combination of two policy measures would be most appropriate for a government to implement. One or both of the policy measures in the distractors may be incorrect.

4 Using your own figures, ask a question requiring students to calculate PED. It would be useful to design the distractors to take into account the mistakes students often make – including, for instance, dividing percentage change in price by percentage change in quantity demanded, and not calculating percentage changes.

5 Select a skilled and an unskilled occupation and ask why the former is better paid than the latter.

6 Use your own figures to test students' awareness that average total cost is total cost divided by output.

7 Taking a particular industry, for instance car production or banking, ask a question requiring students to distinguish between economies of scale and diseconomies of scale.

8 Ask students to identify an invisible export of your country. The distractors may include, for example, a visible export, an invisible import and foreign direct investment overseas.

LOOKING BACK

Using multiple-choice questions in your lessons increases students' skills and enhances their examination performance. Having read this chapter, you may wish to ask yourself the following questions:

- Do you use multiple-choice questions from the start of your course?
- Do you have an adequate supply of multiple-choice questions?
- Do you use a variety of techniques to teach multiple-choice skills?
- Do your students do themselves justice in multiple-choice papers?

6 Structured questions

The nature of structured questions

'Structured questions' is both a general and a specific term. Examination papers entitled 'Structured questions' are usually employing the term in its more general sense. This covers three types of question. These are short questions, structured questions (narrowly defined) and stimulus questions:

- **Short questions** are not necessarily in themselves short. The name derives from the fact that they require short answers. A series of short questions can be on the same or different topics.
- **Structured questions** are short questions on a topic or related topics which usually build up in terms of marks and degree of difficulty. They may be based on a short text, often on a real-world example.
- **Stimulus questions** are often based on a short passage or extract from a newspaper article but they may be based on a diagram. This type of question requires candidates to interpret the data provided. They also often build up in terms of marks and degree of difficulty.

IGCSE and O Level structured question papers

CIE's IGCSE Paper 2 contains one compulsory question in the form of a stimulus question. This has a number of question parts, normally five or six. The paper also requires candidates to answer all of the four structured questions. These questions have a stem of a sentence or two and are based on real-world examples. There are two parts – a and b – to each question.

IGCSE Paper 4 and O Level Paper 2 have a compulsory stimulus question of the same kind as in IGCSE Paper 2. Candidates also have to select three questions from six structured questions. Again, these questions have a stem of one or two sentences, but this time the questions have three or four parts.

General guidance on answering structured questions

For answering any type of structured question, there are certain points to emphasise to students. These include the following:

- Read the question very carefully. For example, if the question asks you to explain two causes of an increase in demand, do not explain one cause or three causes. Also do not just identify two causes. In each case, state a cause and then explain how it would lead to more being demanded.
- Pay particular attention to the number of marks being awarded. These give an indication of the time that should be spent on the question and the length of the answer expected. Students frequently spend too long on the first few questions, which often do not carry many marks. This results in them not having enough time to spend on the analytical (higher mark) questions.
- Answer the questions directly. Make sure that everything you write is relevant.

Student activity 6.1

Arrange the class into small groups of, for example, three to four students. Give out to each group two sets of cards: one with short questions on a given topic and one with suggested answers. Ask each group to:

- match up the questions and answers;
- explain their decisions to the whole group.

Guidance on answering structured questions

In addition to the points mentioned above, explain to students that it is important to:

- read through all the structured parts first;
- bear in mind the general theme(s) of the question – this can help you answer the succeeding questions;
- avoid overlap in answers.

Stimulus questions

Stimulus questions may assess a range of skills, including written communication, knowledge and understanding, analysis, judgement and decision-making. They also require students to handle data, and interpretation is a key element of this type of question. Students have to read any information given carefully, consider its meaning, and decide what Economics concepts they are going to apply in their answers.

They may have to carry out calculations – for example, percentage changes – may have to come to conclusions on the basis of the information given, and are frequently asked to use demand and supply diagrams.

Time can be a factor with this type of paper and some students do run out of time. This makes it very important that students consider very carefully how much time to devote to each question part and follow the directive words carefully.

Developing performance in structured questions

Much of the work that students undertake will hone the skills needed to answer structured questions. From the start of the course, students' interest and awareness of current affairs need to be encouraged. They also need practice in applying their Economics knowledge and understanding to specific questions. Some of these may be based on past examination questions and others on ones you have constructed yourself.

At the beginning, students could be asked to work on questions in small groups and then the answers could be discussed with the whole class. A number of structured questions could be set for homework. As the course progresses, you should give your students plenty of practice in answering structured questions under examination conditions.

One way in which you might want to increase your students' ability to answer structured questions is to ask them to prepare and give presentations on particular economics events. This will increase their ability to apply their Economics knowledge to real-world examples. Allowing other class members to ask them questions on their specialist topics should also sharpen their analytical and evaluative skills.

Constructing short questions

It is relatively easy to construct short questions. These can be used to check understanding at regular intervals. You might want to produce a number of short questions on a topic when you have completed it, and also a number on a range of topics covered at the end of term.

Example 6.1: Short questions

1 Define demand. (2)
2 What is the only cause of an extension in demand? (2)
3 Explain two causes of an increase in demand for rice. (4)
4 What is meant by equilibrium price? (2)
5 What does a supply curve show? (3)
6 Explain two causes of a shift to the left of the supply curve of coffee. (6)
7 What is meant by equilibrium price? (2)
8 Using a diagram, explain the effect of an increase in income on the market for cars. (6)
9 Using a diagram, explain the effect of an increase in the tax on cigarettes. (6)
10 Explain why the price of calculators has fallen in recent years. (4)

Constructing structured questions

In constructing structured questions, it is useful to have a stem of a few sentences based on a recent event.

Example 6.2: Structured questions

1 In 2004 the South Korean economy ran into difficulties. The country's inflation rate rose whilst its economic growth rate fell.
   a) Explain what is meant by a fall in a country's growth rate. (3)
   b) Discuss the costs of inflation. (7)

2 From 2002 to 2004 the value of the currency of the Dominican Republic fell by more than 50 per cent. This increased inflationary pressure but failed to stop the country's balance of payments deficit increasing.
   a) Explain why a fall in the value of a country's currency might increase inflationary pressure. (4)
   b) Discuss why exchange rates fluctuate. (6)

3 Demand for the Mini car, produced by BMW at Oxford in the UK, continued to increase in 2004. It was predicted that the Oxford factory would produce more than 180,000 cars in the year. The factory cannot exceed its capacity of about 200,000 cars without a substantial increase in investment.
   a) Calculate the percentage of spare capacity the factory had in 2004. (2)
   b) Explain what factors might increase demand for a particular model of car. (6)
   c) Discuss the effects that increasing the size of its factory may have on BMW's costs of production. (7)

Teacher activity 6.1

Using recent newspaper articles, construct structured questions on trends in population, international trade and changes in unemployment.

Constructing stimulus questions

Stimulus questions may be based on a newspaper article, an extract from a book, a diagram, a statistical table or a combination of these.

Example 6.3: Stimulus questions

1

Since 1977 Argentina's farmers have more than doubled their crop yields. Soya production has tripled. The crop accounted for a quarter of the country's exports in 2003 and brought the government $1.5 billion in export taxes. Output has increased because of new sowing methods, the application of more fertilisers and the widespread use of genetically modified crops. The soya boom, however, has caused some worries. The price of soya fluctuates on world markets. In 2004 it fell, largely because Chinese consumers switched to other products. Relying on one crop and engaging in less crop rotation also risks exhausting the soil.

a) i What is meant by a tax? (1)
ii Explain two reasons why governments impose taxes. (4)
iii What evidence is there in the extract that soya is an important crop in Argentina? (3)

b) Using demand and supply analysis, explain why the price of soya fell in 2004. (5)

c) Discuss whether an increase in soya production would benefit Argentina. (7)

2

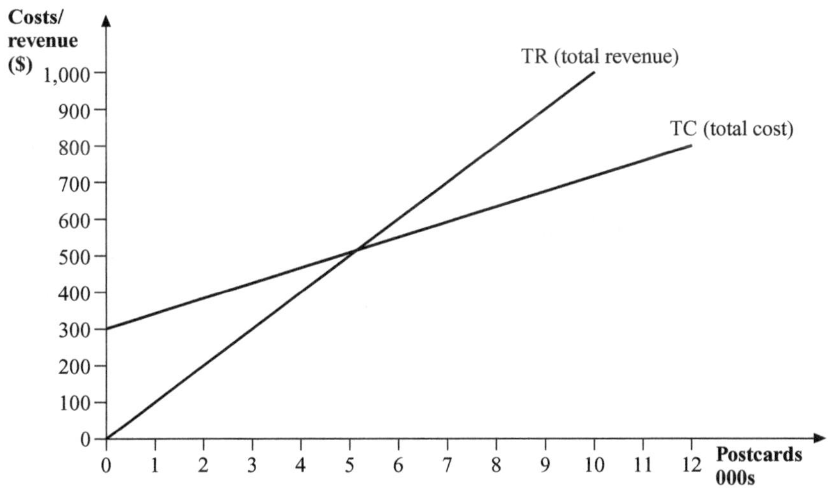

Cost and revenue of a company producing postcards

a) i Define total revenue. (2)
ii What is the break-even level of output? (1)
iii How much does one postcard sell for? (2)

b) i What would be the average cost if 8,000 postcards were sold? (2)
ii Using an example, explain what is meant by a fixed cost. (3)
iii What is the fixed cost and the variable cost of producing 6,000 postcards? (4)

c) Describe two economies of scale a firm producing postcards could gain as it grows in size. (6)

3

Figures for 2000

Country	Population (millions)	GDP per head (US$)	Adult literacy rate (%)
Bangladesh	75.6	1,602	41
Jamaica	2.0	3,639	87
Norway	4.0	29,918	99

a) Explain what is meant by:
i GDP per head (2)
ii adult literacy rate. (2)

b) Calculate the GDP of Jamaica. (2)

c) Explain what relationship you would expect to find between GDP per head and adult literacy rate. (4)

d) Which country's citizens appear to have the highest living standards? Explain your answer. (4)

e) Describe three indicators of living standards not shown in the table. (6)

Student activity 6.2

Divide the class into two to four mixed-ability teams. Ask each team to work on the same stimulus question. They should then report back their answers to a whole-class discussion.

LOOKING BACK

There are a number of points arising from this chapter that you may want to consider:

- When do your students start answering structured questions?
- Do you occasionally allow your students to work in groups on structured questions?
- Do you provide your students with the opportunity to answer a variety of structured questions?

7 Coursework

Why do coursework?

Undertaking coursework increases the motivation of many students. It can give them a real sense of achievement, and many take considerable pride in their work.

For some students who are not good at examinations, coursework can provide the opportunity to shine. It is a different form of assessment, undertaken under different conditions, and it gives students flexibility to work at their own pace.

By its very nature, coursework draws on real-world data, and this helps students to see the relevance of Economics. The opportunity often given to draw on local examples also helps students to relate their studies to a local issue and they can study a topic they enjoy in depth.

When they are developing their coursework skills, students can work cooperatively. Moving on to their individual enquiry, students will develop the ability to work independently.

Coursework does, however, place demands on both teachers and students. It has to be planned and organised carefully, coursework skills have to be developed, students have to be kept motivated, and their work has to be marked and moderated. Nevertheless, many teachers opt for coursework. This is because of the significant rewards that students can gain from doing it. One of the most significant is the opportunity it gives them to work as an economist. The skills and techniques that students employ in coursework are exactly the same as those used by professional economists.

What to consider when introducing coursework

There are a number of points to take into account when deciding to introduce coursework. The most important is the need to include it as an integral part of your scheme of work. Syllabuses emphasise that 'teachers must regard coursework tasks as an integral part of teaching the syllabus and not as a separate entity'. From the start of the course, coursework skills can be developed. Indeed, coverage of the syllabus should inform students' coursework and vice versa. Time spent in guiding and monitoring students should be spread out over the academic year rather than concentrated into a short space of time.

The syllabus has to be checked. A syllabus will spell out carefully the rules and regulations involved. It will provide information on what topics centres can select from and how many words students can be expected to write, advice on how to approach coursework and details of how marks should be awarded, and it will explain how moderation should be carried out.

Resource implications need to be considered. The main requirement is likely to be secondary sources of data, including government statistics, Economics magazines, newspapers and the Internet. Collecting primary data may also give rise to a need for resources – including possibly the use of telephones, notebooks and equipment to draw up and print questionnaires.

Thought has to be given to whether coursework will involve students in activities outside the school, and if so whether any safety or permission issues are involved.

It is also necessary to consider whether your students will cope with coursework. In connection with this, there are a number of key factors to consider. One is whether you have many students who join your course partway through. Another is whether your students are also doing coursework in other subjects. If they are, you should liaise carefully with other teachers involved to spread out deadlines so you avoid overloading students at particular times. You can also check whether the coursework skills your students will be developing in other subjects are relevant to Economics and whether what you will be doing can help them in other areas. It may be possible for the same primary data to be used for coursework in two different subject areas – for example, data on the location of industry could be used in both Economics and Business Studies, and data on social costs and benefits could be used in both Economics and Environmental Studies.

Teacher activity 7.1

List the problems that you think doing coursework may pose and suggest how you might overcome these.

How to approach coursework

There is a logical structure to coursework. Before starting teaching, you have to get approval from the examination board to do coursework. If you are following the IGCSE syllabus, you need to have undertaken the necessary training and CIE has to be assured about your moderating arrangements. Then you have to select the topic or topics from a number given by the examination board. This is a crucial stage. Any topic you select should be one that the students are interested in, that they can apply a significant amount of Economics to, and for which there is a readily available range of primary and secondary data.

After the topic has been selected, students have to decide what data is required. This is obviously easier if they have already been introduced to a variety of sources (see below). It is important that they are focused at this stage as there is a danger that they will try to draw on too much data – they must be selective.

Then students have to collect the data from primary and secondary sources. This is a stage that students often particularly enjoy.

Having collected the data, they need to sort it out and to analyse it. Analysis is an important stage, drawing on economic theories and concepts, and often receives the highest proportion of the total marks.

The final two stages are evaluation and presentation. Evaluation involves assessing the data and coming to some decision or judgement. Students should aim for clear presentation. Most students take considerable care over presentation. This is good, but it is important that they get the balance right. A well-presented piece of coursework lacking relevant analysis and evaluation will not gain many marks.

Example 7.1 shows a model for coursework proposed for the IGCSE Economics syllabus.

Example 7.1: Coursework model

Selecting e.g. identification of data that need to be collected

↓

Collection e.g. use of primary and/or secondary sources

↓

Sorting e.g. sampling, ordering, tabulating relevant facts, figures etc.

↓

Analysis e.g. statistical manipulation, application of theories, ideas

↓

Evaluation e.g. identifying and testing statements of opinion, making decisions and judgements on the topic

↓

Presentation e.g. logical layout and a variety of presentation techniques

Teacher activity 7.2

Check the syllabus to see what topics students can do for coursework. Then consider:

- where your students' interests lie;
- the key questions involved in the topic you are thinking of selecting;
- what Economics concepts can be applied to the topic;
- when your students will have received sufficient basic instruction in the topic;
- what skills would be developed in the topic.

Student activity 7.1

Ask students as a group how they would plan the following investigations:

- variations in the price of fish in a local market;
- whether nurses should be paid more than footballers;
- how significant the primary sector is in the local area;
- the total cost of congestion in the local area.

Developing coursework skills

The skills needed to carry out coursework should be developed from the start of the course. They include the ability to undertake independent research into sources of data, to interpret data, to apply economic concepts and theories, to solve problems, to write clearly, to use a range of different presentation techniques, and to evaluate.

Coursework may draw on a number of numerical skills. Students may have to use diagrams and to calculate averages, totals and percentages; and some investigations may require them to create an index.

Carrying out coursework

As the IGCSE syllabus emphasises, it is important to ensure that 'candidates have received sufficient basic instructions in the course, and in the context of a particular syllabus theme, before they commence the coursework topic'.

It is useful to break down the coursework into sections with interim deadlines. This will help you to monitor the students' work and to maintain their interest.

Collecting data

As mentioned above, students can draw on both primary and secondary data. **Secondary data** is information originally collected for other purposes and includes government statistics, magazines and newspaper articles, and Economics dictionaries. **Secondary research**, sometimes called desk research, has the advantage that it can be done relatively quickly and in the classroom.

Collecting primary data is a more time-consuming exercise, but it can be more rewarding. **Primary data** is new information collected for the purpose of the enquiry. Primary data has the advantages that the collector can concentrate specifically on the information they need, and will know exactly where it has come from, the circumstances under which it was collected, and any limitations of the data.

Most students enjoy collecting primary data, and it provides them with the opportunity to develop a range of skills. Among the ways of getting primary data are conducting interviews and drawing up and using questionnaires.

Interviews

Interviews may be conducted over the telephone or by email, but the most informative way is probably face to face. Before students carry out any interview, it is advisable that they practise interviewing each other. This should help them develop the skills of phrasing questions unambiguously, listening and interpreting.

They should then be encouraged to request and conduct interviews in a polite manner, explaining the purpose of the interview. If those who agree to be interviewed have a good experience, they are more likely to be willing to be interviewed in the future.

In the interview students should avoid vague, leading or personal questions, and they should try to keep the interview short.

In those areas where it is not possible to send students out to carry out primary research, alternative arrangements can be made. As well as using the telephone and emails to conduct interviews, family members, friends and fellow students can be asked to be interviewees.

Questionnaires

Questionnaires can be used with interviews or on their own. In drawing up a questionnaire, a number of key points need to be considered:

- Who is the questionnaire aimed at?
- What is the information required?
- How is the information to be used?
- Whether you are going to ask open or closed questions or a mixture.

Open questions permit the respondent to give their own answer. These can provide some useful information, but owing to the potentially large range of answers they may be difficult to analyse. In contrast, **closed questions** are questions that permit only a limited number of responses. Respondents have a choice between a number of alternatives already given. These may be in the form of multiple-choice questions. Closed questions have the advantages of being relatively easy to analyse and of making it easy to capture the information required.

- The need to keep questions short. Most people are busy, and they are more likely to be prepared to answer a questionnaire that will take a relatively short time to answer.
- The advisability of trying out the questionnaire with friends or others in the class to iron out any problems.
- The importance of a clear and attractive layout.
- The arrangements for getting the questionnaires back. For example, if they are to be sent through the post, it is important to include a stamped addressed envelope.
- Whether to allow people to fill in the questionnaire by themselves or whether the students will read out the questions and fill in the answers. The latter has the benefit that, if necessary, questions can be explained, and it overcomes the problem of getting the questionnaire back.
- The need to ensure that the questionnaire is given to a representative sample of the target population. An unrepresentative sample will distort findings. For example, sending out questionnaires by email will give a biased result if most of the target population do not have access to email.

When writing up the coursework, it is important for students to comment on how they have collected the data and on any shortcomings and strengths of the data.

Student activity 7.2

Ask students to construct a questionnaire to find out what factors influence people's choice of occupation.

Presentation of the data

In coursework, it is useful to include a variety of ways of presenting data. As well as written comments, tables, graphs, diagrams and maps may be used.

Tables and graphs should have clear titles which indicate what they show, and their sources should be given. Tables should be arranged in columns and rows which have clear labels. They are useful in showing the relationship between two sets of statistics – for instance, unemployment and inflation percentages – although a scatter diagram could also be used.

Graphs, including pie charts and bar graphs, look attractive and may show data in a memorable and easily understood way. Students, however, should be warned against cluttering their graphs.

Maps are useful to include in coursework based on a study of a local area.

Completing the coursework

The coursework should have a clear and relevant title. There should be a succinct introduction, which should state the aim of the enquiry and discuss the approach used.

It should be presented in a logical manner. The writing should be lucid, correctly spelled and grammatically correct. It should be well structured. Points should follow on naturally from the previous ones. Headings and subheadings can be used to break down the text and indicate the key areas.

The conclusion should summarise the main findings, bringing out key evaluative points. At the end a list of references can be given.

Performing well at coursework

There are a number of keys to doing coursework:

- Choose a topic which is manageable and for which data is readily available.
- Pose a clear question.
- Plan the work carefully by breaking up the coursework into manageable portions, capable of being monitored.
- Identify time limits for the completion of each discrete task.
- Select data very carefully, making sure it is relevant and up to date.
- Apply relevant Economics concepts and theories.
- Work out a logical structure.
- Use a variety of ways of presenting data.
- Ensure your analysis and evaluation are supported by the data you have selected.
- Conclude with a clear summary of the question posed.

Assessing coursework

Examination boards give guidance on how coursework should be assessed. They state the number of marks to be awarded for each of the skills assessed and provide advice on how to award the marks. For example, top marks are awarded in IGCSE Economics for:

- well-designed research carried out effectively, fully investigating the economic problem or situation and collecting all the relevant information (Selection and collection of data, 9–10 marks);

- information collected is fully and clearly displayed, using a complete and appropriate range of presentation skills (Presentation of relevant data, 5 marks);
- evidence of original and clear analysis of the topic, with relevant and accurate use of economic ideas (Analysis and interpretation of the topic, 13–15 marks);
- a reasoned and justified conclusion based on the evidence collected and a clear answer to the question posed in the title (Evaluation of the topic, 9–10 marks).

Moderation

Moderation is a key aspect of the process. It is important that all candidates in a centre are marked to the same standard.

If there are several teachers in your centre, it is necessary to carry out internal moderation. In this process, teachers could first mark a sample of their own students' coursework. They then bring these along to a team meeting and discuss how they arrived at the marks. Colleagues could then check each other's marks. After the meeting, teachers could mark their remaining students' coursework. Then 'blind' marking could be used. This involves, firstly, a teacher marking their own students' coursework, and then another colleague or colleagues marking the work without knowing what mark the original teacher gave. Any differences in marks should be fully explored before a final mark is arrived at.

Alternative to coursework

For a variety of reasons, centres may opt for the alternative to coursework. In this case, students should still develop enquiry skills. This will help them not only with the alternative to the coursework paper, but also with other papers. It should make the course more interesting and relevant.

Carrying out an investigation will strengthen students' ability to analyse and evaluate; increase their understanding of tables, graphs and diagrams; and raise their awareness of the information needed to investigate different issues.

Students could carry out much or all of the work in the classroom, drawing on secondary data. They could be set two or three investigations and/or a number of exercises in research work.

Some of the tasks, particularly the collection of data, could be undertaken as a group activity; whilst the presentation, analysis and evaluation of the data could be done on an individual basis.

Student activity 7.3

In groups, ask students to identify what information would be needed to decide whether:

- a merger would be beneficial;
- people have a better standard of living now than 30 years ago;
- tax revenue should be spent on building a new museum or a school;
- a firm operates in a competitive market;
- the main factors that influence consumers' demand for rail transport;
- the effect of an increase in tourism on local people.

LOOKING BACK

Coursework enables students to work as economists and increases their skills and motivation. In reviewing this chapter you might want to consider the following:

- What are the main factors influencing whether you do coursework?
- What do you think is the most demanding stage of coursework?
- How could your students benefit more from undertaking coursework activities?
- Are there local sources that can be drawn on for coursework?
- Does coursework seem to be an attractive alternative to an examination assessment?
- Do you have experience at internal moderation?

8 Revision strategies and examination preparation

Some students fail to do themselves justice in examinations because of a lack of revision. Even more, however, fail to get the grades their ability justifies because of inappropriate revision.

It is important to emphasise to students that revision is a continuous process. It should start at the beginning of the course, not be confined to a few weeks before the examination. You should stress that it is quality and not quantity of revision that matters.

Stages of revision

Revising work just before an examination will not be effective. Students should be encouraged to see revision as a process of checking, deepening and consolidating their knowledge and understanding, and not as cramming. They should be encouraged to undertake revision in stages. After each lesson they should review the work they have done and the notes they have taken. You can help this process by starting each lesson with a recap of the previous lesson's work, asking students about the work covered and encouraging them to ask about anything they have not understood.

At the end of each week, each month and each term, they should then review their work again. At this stage, they should add to their notes where appropriate, ensure they understand the work fully and can explain it in their own words, and engage in active revision.

Approximately a month before the examination starts, the last stage of revision should occur. This is the most intensive stage and involves consolidation. If students have followed a progressive course of revision, checking and processing their work three or four times before, this stage should consist of their reviewing work they are familiar with and which they fully understand.

Student activity 8.1

Ask students to draw up a study plan for the next month, indicating when they plan to revise.

Active revision

The least productive, but frequently used, revision strategy is to read through notes passively. This is not an effective use of time and can be quite boring. What students should engage in is active revision. As its name suggests, this involves actively doing something to reinforce understanding. Such active revision can take a number of forms, including summarising notes, producing tables, drawing spider diagrams, practising diagrams, checking out directive words, taking part in tests and quizzes, and sitting a mock examination.

Summarising notes

This is probably the most traditional and common form of active learning. Students should select the most important points. These can be cross-referenced, perhaps by using colour coding.

Tables

These are a useful way of processing information and making links. For example, the following table could be drawn up on demand and supply:

	Demand	**Supply**
Definition	Willingness and ability to buy a product	Willingness and ability to sell a product
Main influences on	Price, income and price of related products	Price, costs of production and technology
Shape of curve	Downward sloping from left to right	Upward sloping from left to right
Effect of an increase	A rise in price and an increase in the quantity traded	A fall in price and an increase in the quantity traded
Effect of a decrease	A fall in price and a fall in the quantity traded	A rise in price and a fall in the quantity traded

Spider diagrams

I particularly like spider diagrams. A central topic or part of a topic is placed in the centre and connected points lead off. This is useful in checking memory and understanding linked points. For example, the spider diagram in Figure 8.1 could be used to summarise the key features of a planned economy.

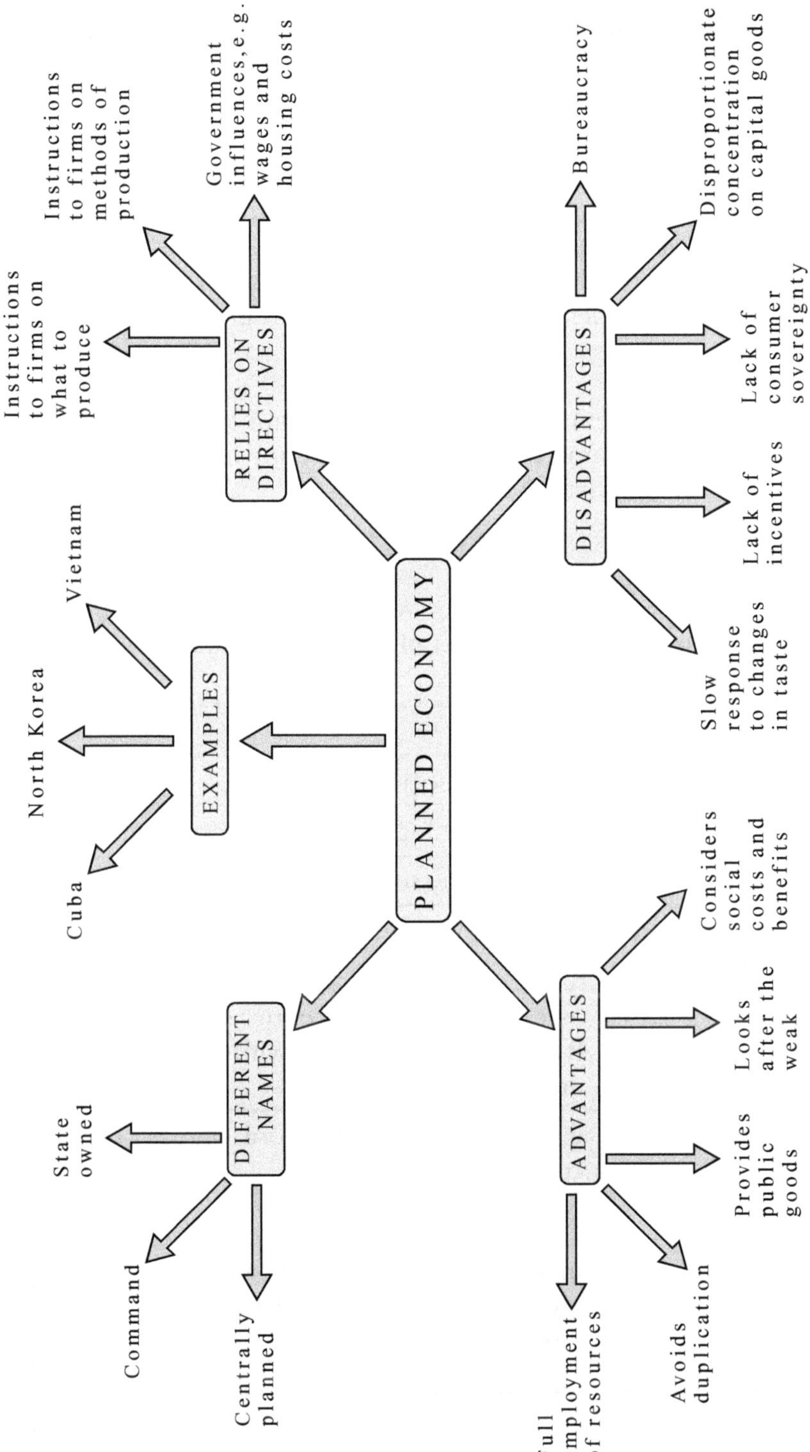

Figure 8.1: A planned economy

Student activity 8.2

Ask students to complete a spider diagram on a market economy.

Diagrams

Students need to check what diagrams they may be expected to draw in examinations. To help understand and memorise these diagrams, they need to practise them. They can include them on revision cards and in answers to worksheets, assignments, tests and mock examination questions. You could also encourage students to place them on walls in their bedrooms.

Directive words

It is important that students understand what examination questions are asking them to do. Reinforce and recap their knowledge of **directive words** (also called command words).

Teacher activity 8.1

Write or type the following directive words on a set of cards of one colour and their definitions on a set of a different colour. Ask students, in groups, to match these.

analyse	explain
apply	use in a specific way
calculate	work out using the information provided
comment on	give your reasoned opinion on
compare / compare and contrast	discuss similarities and differences between
criticise	assess the merits of theories or opinions, backing the assessment with evidence and reasoning
define	give the meaning of a word, phrase or concept
describe	give a detailed account of
discuss	investigate or examine by argument, giving reasons for and against, and discussing implications
distinguish between or differentiate	look for differences between

evaluate	assess an argument, weighing up arguments for and against
explain	make plain, interpret, give reasons for
identify	select, point out
illustrate	explain or clarify, using examples
justify	show adequate reasons for decisions or conclusions, making out a case and answering the main objections which may be made
outline	briefly describe the main features
state	make clear
to what extent	make a judgement

Tests

Regular tests, including some past examination questions, can be used to build up students' understanding and memory. These also enable you to find out common areas of misunderstanding and to provide useful feedback.

Quizzes

Quizzes are a fun way of encouraging students to revise. Students tend to be competitive and they usually enjoy quizzes. The class can be divided into teams, each with a captain. Two points are awarded for a correct answer. If a team gets a question wrong, it is passed to the next team, who get one point for a correct answer.

Last-stage revision

This stage should involve students re-examining, reconsidering and applying information, concepts and theories they have already understood and learned.

Students should be encouraged to draw up a revision plan for this period, covering all the subjects they are studying and broken down into manageable chunks. It should include not only what is to be revised and when, but also what revision strategies will be employed. It is important that the students are realistic in what they are setting themselves to achieve. Many students get despondent because their plans are over-ambitious.

The revision sessions should be broken down into short periods with breaks. Short revision periods of between 15 and 30 minutes will prove much more effective than long periods. Time should be allowed for other activities and flexibility should be built into the plan. Students should revise in a place as free from distractions as possible.

At this stage of revision, practising answering past examination questions to time is a particularly useful exercise. You may wish to hold a full mock examination. This would enable students to experience examination conditions and provide you with information about individual and group performance. It may also result in your adapting your revision programme.

In addition to undertaking the active revision activities already mentioned, it is useful for students to test each other. Both the one being tested and the one asking the questions gains by reviewing their work and discussing the answers.

Revision dos and don'ts

There are certain key dos and don'ts to stress to students.

Dos

- Do engage in active and purposeful revision.
- Do revise throughout the course.
- Do use a variety of revision activities.
- Do reward yourself after successful periods of revision.
- Do make sure you understand all your work as you go along.
- Do go to bed early the night before the examination.

Don'ts

- Don't revise when tired.
- Don't revise for long periods.
- Don't leave revision to the last few weeks before the examination (panic revision).
- Don't revise just by reading through notes passively.

Examination techniques

Having undertaken sound revision, it is important that this is put to good use in the examination. There are a number of key pieces of advice to give to students:

Dos

- Have a good night's sleep the night before the examination.
- Make sure you know where the examination is to be held.
- Check before the examination on the format of the paper, the number of questions and whether there is a choice.

- Make sure that you take all the necessary equipment to the examination – pens, pencils, erasers, rulers, sharpeners and calculators.
- Arrive at least ten minutes before the start.
- Read and follow the instructions on the front of the paper carefully.
- Check key directive words. It may be useful to highlight these.
- Carefully work out what the questions are asking.
- If there is a choice of questions, check which you can do best. If there are two parts to a question, make sure you can do both parts.
- Put the number of the question you are answering in the left-hand column.
- Allocate your time appropriately. The number of marks given to each question is a guide to how long you should spend on it.
- Think through your answers before you start writing them. This will avoid your jumping from one point to another.
- Answer questions directly.
- Glance back to the question from time to time, to ensure that you are still answering it in a relevant way.
- Leave space at the end of each question in case you think of something to add later.
- Make sure that any diagrams you draw are clear, approximately a third of a page in size, accurately labelled and referred to in the text of your answer.
- Explain the Economics terms you use. Write as if you are explaining something to an intelligent but uninformed reader.
- Remember that, unless you are asked to, answering in note form will not gain high marks. Wherever possible, write in sentences. The only time you should resort to writing a list is if you are running out of time.
- Leave time at the end to read through your answers.

Don'ts

- Don't write out the question.
- Don't start answering questions straightaway.
- Don't rush your answers.
- Don't use correcting fluid.
- Don't squeeze in material you have left out. Put in an asterisk where the material should go and write it where there is space.
- Don't make your diagrams too small or too cluttered.
- Don't answer more questions than required.

Student activity 8.3

In a group, ask students what has gone right and what has gone wrong in past examinations, and what lessons can be learned from their experience.

Common errors

There are some general mistakes and some specific errors that students make in Economics examinations.

The **general mistakes** include being ill-prepared due to a lack of revision, misreading instructions, misinterpreting questions, failing to answer all the questions and running out of time.

There is a range of **specific mistakes**. A common one is for students to confuse percentage and absolute changes. This leads them to misinterpret a fall in the rate of inflation as a fall in the general price level and a fall in the economic growth rate as a fall in output.

A number of Economics concepts are commonly confused. These include:

- a budget deficit and a balance of payments deficit;
- public corporations and public limited companies;
- productivity and production;
- a contraction and a decrease in demand;
- inelastic demand and perfectly inelastic demand;
- investment and saving;
- social costs and external costs.

A significant number of students lose marks because they make mistakes on diagrams. These mistakes include confusing demand and supply curves, showing a decrease in supply by shifting the supply curve to the right rather than to the left, and labelling the vertical axis as supply and the horizontal axis as demand.

It is very useful to check mark schemes and examiners' reports. These provide clear guidance on what is required and include comments on common errors.

Student activity 8.4

Ask the class to consider the statements below and discuss to what extent they agree with them:

1. It is best to plan to use every spare hour to revise.
2. It is best to revise on your own.
3. It is best to work long sessions on revision without a break.
4. A revision timetable will tie you down too much.

5 It is best to build variety into your revision.
6 It is best to work very hard on the night before an examination.
7 Last-minute revision is the most effective.
8 You should revise hardest for your best subject.
9 It is best to ask yourself questions as you revise.
10 You should allow yourself time between revision activities for social activities.

(When discussing these points afterwards, remember that the most effective revision strategy for individual students will vary somewhat.)

LOOKING BACK

For students to achieve their potential, it is crucial that they engage in purposeful and active revision, prepare appropriately for their examinations and avoid common errors. You may wish to ask yourself the following questions:

- Do my students engage in revision from the start of their course?
- What methods could I use to encourage my students to engage in active revision?
- Do I check that my students draw up revision plans?
- What advice do I give to my students about examination technique?
- How could I help my students avoid making common errors?

9 Resources

In selecting the resources to use in your teaching, there are a number of factors to bear in mind. One is the financial constraints placed on you by your school budget. Others are that the resources should match the needs and abilities of your students, and that you need to keep resources up to date. Fortunately there are a variety of resources that can be used to develop students' skills and to make Economics lessons stimulating and interesting.

Newspaper and magazine articles

I find newspaper and magazine articles particularly useful. I use them in a variety of ways – for instance, as the basis for worksheets, in wall displays, in preparation of case studies and for my own research. They provide up-to-date information about changes in economic policies, current economic issues and developments in economic theory.

I collect articles on a variety of topics myself, and I encourage my students to read articles in a quality newspaper and, if possible, to keep a scrapbook of relevant ones. I also buy a class copy of *Economics Today* and *The Economic Review* – although these are designed for AS and A Level students. To keep myself up to date with developments in the economy and economic theory, I buy the *Financial Times* newspaper and *The Economist* magazine. Through membership of the Economics and Business Education Association, I receive the journal *Teaching Business and Economics*, which provides useful advice and ideas on teaching Economics. For example, it provides up-to-date information on websites, as well as suggestions on role playing and other activities that can be used to enhance learning.

Textbooks

A student textbook is a major resource. It can be used in classroom activities, for homework assignments, as a source for notes and as a reference. Textbooks, however, are expensive to buy – especially if you update the class text every few years. It is important, therefore, to ensure that you buy the best textbook possible and that you and your students make full and appropriate use of it.

If finances permit, you may be able to buy additional books that can supplement the main textbook in terms of coverage, approach or exercises. You may also be able to afford an Economics dictionary that can be used for reference purposes.

Teacher activity 9.1

In deciding which textbook to buy, consider the following points:

- Does the book cover the syllabus you follow?
- Is the book accessible to your students in terms of language and complexity?
- Does the book include multiple-choice questions, short questions and other exercises?
- Can the book be used by students for homework assignments?
- Is the book up to date?
- Does the book have an attractive layout?
- Are the diagrams clear, accurate and well labelled?
- Does the book make use of real-world examples?
- Is there a glossary at the end of the book?
- Is there a clear and accurate index?
- Does the book provide value for money?

Statistical sources

A range of statistical information is provided by governments and their agencies and by other bodies. In the UK the Office for National Statistics (ONS), for instance, publishes the *Annual Abstract of Statistics* (giving annual figures and trends over the last ten years on, for example, population, GDP, unemployment, inflation and balance of payments), the *Monthly Digest of Statistics* (providing up-to-date information on similar areas) and *Social Trends* (covering information on housing, transport, income distribution, earnings and so on).

Statistical information is also provided by the quality newspapers, the European Union, the International Monetary Fund and the United Nations. I find the tables in the UN's *Human Development Report* a particularly useful source of information about economic development in the world's economies.

Free resources

A number of free resources are available, including bank bulletins and reviews, budget and pre-budget reports, support material provided by the examination board, reports from companies, and material specially designed by companies for Economics students.

Many free resources are useful in keeping you up to date and providing you with the basis for active learning activities. It is important to remember, however, that just because the resources are free, that does not mean that you have to use them. As with any resource, you need to consider their quality, appropriateness and accessibility.

Television programmes and videos/DVDs

A number of programmes and videos/DVDs can provide the basis for learning activities. These include news programmes, current affairs programmes and some specialist Economics programmes.

In using this type of resource, however, care has to be taken. If shown relatively long programmes and/or required to watch without any clear focus, students tend to become bored and easily distracted. It is better to show programmes in short sections and set students specific tasks on them. These may include, for instance, question-and-answer sessions, worksheets and discussions based on the extracts. Such extracts can also be used in case studies and in role playing, and to provide background information for coursework.

As well as using programmes in class, I encourage students to watch current affairs programmes and to watch the news regularly.

Radio

Whilst not providing visual images, radio programmes are good at developing listening skills. News programmes and programmes focusing on issues such as changes in interest rates, the role of trade unions and the environment can be used in similar ways to television programmes.

Information and communications technology

ICT is developing all the time, providing a range of resources for students and teachers. The price of hardware and software is falling, making ICT accessible to more schools and students. Nevertheless, your use of ICT will clearly be influenced by what facilities are available in your school, and by your and your students' ICT skills.

When using ICT in the classroom, it is important to ensure that all students have the skills and opportunity to use the equipment. Where students' ICT skills vary and/or where the number of computers is limited, you may wish to set group tasks. Another way to approach such a situation is to set differentiated work, some of which requires the use of ICT and some of which does not. The intention would be that all students could gain a sense of achievement and that students would not be sitting idle and waiting for equipment to become free.

In some countries all students and teachers are given email addresses. This enables teachers to keep in contact with students, and students with each other. As noted in Chapter 7, students can use email to contact people in connection with their coursework. For example, they may send a questionnaire to a number of local firms about their locational decisions. Email can also facilitate contact between teachers in different schools.

The use of ICT allows students to carry out a number of other activities. They can word process some of their work and can use it to produce graphs and spreadsheets.

ICT is a useful resource for both teachers and students. It can provide you with a wide range of information, including access to newspaper articles, magazine articles, material from the examination board and learning materials. It makes it easier and quicker to update your class materials, including worksheets, and you may be able to use, for example, PowerPoint in introducing topics to the class.

Teacher activity 9.2

Using email, set up a support group with other Economics teachers so that you can share information and ideas about learning activities and assessment.

Student activity 9.1

Ask students to research a number of websites and report back to the class on their usefulness. For instance:

- www.bized.ac.uk
- bbc.co.uk/knowledge/economics
- www.europe-economist.com/
- www.un.org

Student activity 9.2

Using a range of ICT – including commercially produced Economics software and the Internet, and newspaper articles, magazine articles, television and radio news programmes – produce a report on the government's budget.

People

People can prove to be a very useful resource. Local business people, civil servants, politicians, school governors and members of pressure groups can be interviewed or sent questionnaires in connection with students' coursework and can be invited to talk to the class.

Some teachers of other subjects may be able to contribute to your classes. For example, a Business Studies teacher may be willing and able to talk about the aims of advertising, and another teacher may be able to provide some insights into the economy of a country they have recently visited.

You may also try to involve parents actively. You could invite them to a meeting in which you explain the work their children will be doing and the skills they will be developing. You could then ask them to encourage their children to watch current affairs programmes, read a quality newspaper, and work hard on their homework. You might also be able to recruit some of them to help with coursework, give talks and perhaps to show your students round their places of work.

Teacher activity 9.3

Carry out an audit of the human resources available to you. Think of ways in which you could make use of these resources.

LOOKING BACK

The effective use of resources can stimulate students, develop their skills and improve their examination performance. You may wish to consider the following questions:

- Do you use a variety of resources?
- Are the resources you use accessible to your students?
- Do you regularly update your resources?
- Are there any ways in which you could make better use of your existing resources?
- Are you happy with the textbook you are currently using?
- Are your ICT skills adequate? If not, are there opportunities available to you to improve them?

10 Conclusion

This book has sought to provide you with a variety of strategies to promote active learning in Economics and thereby to increase the enjoyment and sense of achievement you and your students gain. Gaining an understanding of Economics and developing the skills of an economist will bring many benefits to your students. They will gain some useful knowledge, develop a range of useful and transferable skills, and enhance their employment and pay prospects; and they may develop a life-long interest in the subject.

Teacher activity 10.1

Organise a poster competition among students approaching the end of their course. Ask them to illustrate what Economics means to them. The best posters can be displayed and discussed with new students.

As a teacher you should not see yourself as just a transmitter of information. Performing such a role puts pressure on you and is often not very effective in developing the performance of individual students. Most of the responsibility of finding out and processing information on the course content should be placed on the students. Your role is more challenging, but also more interesting. It includes keeping up to date with developments in the subject, promoting your students' learning through a range of stimulating activities, and assessing their progress.

Teaching a motivated group of students, each making good progress, is a very rewarding experience. I hope this book will help you achieve that.

Appendix A: useful sources of information

Textbooks

There are currently not many textbooks available that have been written specifically for IGCSE/O level students. Among those intended for this market are the following:

- Alain Anderton, *Economics for GCSE* (1999), Collins Education. This includes data response questions.
- Dan Moynihan and Brian Titley, *Economics: A Complete Course* (3rd edition, 2000), Oxford University Press. This covers the course quite well and includes data response material.

Some teachers may wish to stretch their more able students by using textbooks designed for AS Level students. These include:

- Colin Bamford (ed.), *Economics for AS* (2nd edition, 2003), Cambridge University Press.
- Susan Grant, *AS Economics* (2003), Longman.

CD-ROMs

There is a CD-ROM, *Nuffield Economics and Business, ICT Investigations*, that includes a particularly good unit on globalisation. It is available from Statistics for Education, 5 Bridge Street, Bishop's Stortford, Hertfordshire CM23 2JU, UK. A number of newspapers produce CD-ROMs, with full text of back issues; these include the *Financial Times*, the *Guardian* and *The Times*.

The Internet

Two useful search engines are:

- www.google.com
- www.yahoo.com

There is also:

- www.estima.com/weblinks.htm – links to economics resources sites.

General websites

- www.bized.ac.uk – Biz/ed; a free information service. It provides key economic statistics, company information, case studies, PowerPoint presentations, lesson plans and assignments.
- www.bized.ac.uk/virtual/economy/index.htm – this site contains information on macroeconomic policy and includes a model which

enables students to input data and to see the impact of the changes in tax policy on the economy.

- www.bbc.co.uk – BBC, a good website for news and education.
- www.bbc.co.uk/schools/gcsebitesize/business/ – a good revision site.
- www.ebea.org.uk – EBEA; this provides advice, contacts and student activities.
- www.economist.com – this includes the current week's issue of *The Economist*, book reviews, surveys and links to related sites.

United Kingdom

- www.bankofengland.co.uk – Bank of England; among the information included on this website is an explanation of the Monetary Policy Committee's interest rate decisions.
- www.ifs.org – Institute of Fiscal Studies; this includes analysis of current fiscal policy and fiscal policy issues.
- www.niesr.ac.uk – National Institute of Economic and Social Research (NIESR); a good source of information for teachers on current economic policy and performance issues, contains good comparative statistical data.
- www.ons.gov.uk – Office for National Statistics; a very good source of statistical data.
- www.hm-treasury.gov.uk – Treasury; provides a range of macroeconomic information, particularly on fiscal policy.
- www.tuc.org.uk – Trades Union Congress (TUC); includes information about labour markets.

Other countries

- www.boj.or.jp/en/index.htm – Bank of Japan; English language site on a central bank that has been seeking to tackle a range of monetary policy problems.
- www.gov.bw – government of Botswana; useful information on an African country that is performing well.
- www.finance.gov.pk – government of Pakistan; contains information about the economic performance and policies of Pakistan.
- www.census.gov/statab/www/ – statistical abstract of the United States; contains a collection of statistics on social and economic conditions in the US.

International

- www.commonwealth.org.uk – Commonwealth organisation; good site for information about the economic performance of different countries, as well as more general information.

- www.europa.eu.int/comm/eurostat – Eurostat; contains useful statistical data on the European Union.
- www.imf.org – International Monetary Fund (IMF); includes a wide range of information on the role of the IMF and current problems faced by members.
- www.oecd.org – Organisation for Economic Co-operation and Development (OECD); provides a considerable amount of information about the economic performance of different countries.
- www.un.org – United Nations (UN); includes information about the activities of the UN and some useful information about economic development.
- www.worldbank.org – World Bank; contains information about the role of the World Bank and its current activities.
- www.wto.org – World Trade Organization (WTO); provides details of the WTO in connection with trade and trade policy.

Appendix B: glossary

Here is a list of important words or terms used in this book with which you should be familiar.

active learning	using teaching styles which involve students participating fully in learning activities
aim	the educational purpose of a course of study
assessment	judgement of abilities, progress and achievement
case studies	information on a current economic issue, with questions
coursework	work carried out by students, often as part of an external qualification, which is assessed by the teacher and moderated by the examination board
curriculum	a course of study
curriculum planning	preparation of programme, covering course content, learning activities and assessment strategies
differentiation	an approach designed to maximise the learning potential of all students
directive word	a word in an examination question giving students instruction
formative assessment	assessment which is designed to inform future teaching and learning by giving feedback to students and teachers
Information and Communications Technology (ICT)	media such as computers, including the Internet
moderation	checking of the marking of students' work to ensure a consistent standard

multiple-choice questions	questions which contain a stem and a number of possible answers, of which only one is correct
self-assessment	judgement made by students on their own performance and progress
structured questions	questions divided into parts, that build up in difficulty
summative assessment	assessment which appraises learning at the end of a course
teaching strategy	an approach designed to facilitate learning
worksheets	sheets of information with questions for students to complete

Index

Other titles in the Professional Development for Teachers series

Teaching and Assessing Skills in Accounting	978-0-521-54367-5
Teaching and Assessing Skills in Business Studies	978-0-521-54366-8
Teaching and Assessing Skills in Computer Studies	978-0-521-75360-9
Teaching and Assessing Skills in English as a Second Language	978-0-521-75356-2
Teaching and Assessing Skills in First Language English	978-0-521-75355-5
Teaching and Assessing Skills in Foreign Languages	978-0-521-60103-0
Teaching and Assessing Skills in Geography	978-0-521-75357-9
Teaching and Assessing Skills in Mathematics	978-0-521-75361-6
Teaching and Assessing Practical Skills in Science	978-0-521-75359-3

Lightning Source UK Ltd.
Milton Keynes UK
UKHW02f1101281117
313493UK00006B/665/P

9 780521 548250